BRITISH LABOR
and
PUBLIC OWNERSHIP

Gaitskell: "If only I hadn't to carry all this—a cartoon by Cummings in the London Sunday Express.

BRITISH LABOR

and

PUBLIC OWNERSHIP

By Herbert E. Weiner

INTRODUCTION BY MICHAEL ROSS

Public Affairs Press, Washington, D. C.

TO MY PARENTS

Printed in the United States of America
Library of Congress Catalog Card No. 59-15840

INTRODUCTION

Britain's labor movement has, in effect, declared a moratorium on new commitments for nationalization. Through its two main bodies, the Trades Union Congress (TUC) and the Labor Party, British labor has established a framework through which it reorganizes its ideas of public ownership and works out practicable programs acceptable to the nation as a whole.

The merits and shortcomings of public ownership as a method of operating and developing modern industry have roused public controversy in Britain and elsewhere for years. The debates became more intense after World War II as the Labor Government began putting into effect the extensive nationalization program to which it had pledged itself during the 1945 general election. The application of the long-evolving nationalization program gave rise to considerable rethinking within the political and industrial wings of British organized labor.

Dr. Weiner has traced through the policies of the TUC the evolution of the idea of nationalization as an objective of British trade unionism, rather than as a goal of partisan political or ideological conviction. He does not debate the merits of nationalization nor pass judgment on the validity or consistency of the trade union view on this controversial issue, but rather seeks to analyze the environment and ideas which have governed the attitudes of British trade unionism towards the public ownership of certain industries and services for the past ninety years.

The TUC holds a commanding position among the trade union movements of the world, especially among those which share its basic conviction that trade unions should aspire to long-range goals beyond day-to-day gains. The TUC is looked upon as a pathfinder by other non-revolutionary trade union movements which have been attracted by ideas that social and economic justice may require the expropriation of private property.

In terms of political philosophy, the principles and methods of nationalization adopted by the TUC assumed a special significance, since international socialists regarded industrialized Britain as a prototype of modern capitalist development. In this context, the experience of the British labor movement became a test as to whether basic economic and social changes could be effected through the exercise of the traditional functions of independent trade unionism and parliamentary democracy. This has significance not only for the highly industrialized economies, but more so for the economically underdeveloped areas and particularly the impressionable new nations where problems of the role of social control and ownership are intimately tied to the aspirations for industrialization in a free society.

The aftermath of British labor's third successive general election defeat in 1959 emphasized the importance of these questions. The outcome of the election demonstrated the fundamental nature of the problem faced by British labor in bringing its program into line with social and economic development. The impact of labor's defeat in Britain was felt throughout the international socialist movement, especially in Europe and Asia. It was clear that social changes had affected the character and composition of British society in a way that was increasingly depriving British labor of its traditional support. In this connection though British labor avoided as much as possible discussing nationalization during the campaign, the issue remained in the public mind as an identification mark to distinguish the Labor Party, to its disadvantage, from the Liberals or Conservatives.

Dr. Weiner's study should contribute significantly toward clarifying the thinking on the controversial questions of public ownership and the goals of organized labor generally. By the apparently simple device of tracing the record and letting it speak for itself his analysis, based on an intimate personal knowledge of the subject, makes clear the extent of popular misconception as to the actual, rather than the ideal relationship between trade unionism, socialism and public ownership.

A similar approach measuring trade union traditions against the record with respect to issues such as equal pay for equal work and the concept of a common bond among the workers of the world might well lead to some enlightening surprises as does this analysis of public ownership. This would be a real service to organized labor as well as to the public.

MICHAEL ROSS

Director, Department of International Affairs
American Federation of Labor-Congress of Industrial Organizations

PREFACE

The ideas and orientation for this volume took root sometime after World War II. Through unexpected good fortune, the author found himself assigned to London and in the position of intimately observing and analyzing the nationalization and post-war reconstruction programs of the Attlee Labor government. Subsequent continuous association with the issues and personalities in British labor provided the stimulus and the opportunities for acquiring the insight for an examination of the sources and motives of British labor's, and particularly of British trade unionism's, attachment to the idea of public ownership.

Some aspect of public ownership touches almost everyone's life in Britain. It is a topic of broad public interest as well as one of special concern to organized labor. In every general election nationalization is a traditional issue. Directly and by implication it has its own peculiar impact on the behavior of the electorate, for it serves to distinguish the basic orientation between the main contenders for power, the Labor Party and the Conservatives. In more recent years nationalization, once a vote-getter for the Labor Party, has become a vote loser. In the last general election it was an issue which Labor Party muted to the extent that it was permitted to do so by its own more doctrinaire socialist elements and by the Conservatives.

Ideas of dramatic social action to remedy the undesirable features of modern western industrialism have colored the thinking of labor-minded organizations throughout the world. In the United States the trade unions debated and disputed for years the British trade union view of society as symbolized by nationalization. Now the doubts that British trade unionism is having about a conception, so central to its socialistic philosophy assumes a particular pertinence for the American trade unions inasmuch as the Americans themselves are re-examining many of their traditions with respect to the political and social roles of trade unions. A similar process of re-examination is underway within the labor movements in other western industrialized countries and this has stirred parallel comparisons with the British scene. This is the case with the German social democrats who have shed some of their traditional Marxian conceptions of public ownership. However, in the economically underdeveloped new nations, nationalization is considered as a sort of touchstone of progressive thinking. It has become associated with national aspirations and pride, and more importantly with the whole question as to whether industrialization can be achieved under government sponsorship within the framework of political democracy.

The author wishes to express his gratitude to many in Britain and the United States who gave invaluable assistance while this work was evolving. Special acknowledgement must be made to Professors Leo Wolman and Aaron Warner of Columbia University; to the U.S. Bureau of Labor Statistics, Mr. Ewan Clague, Commissioner, and Mrs. Aryness Joy Wickens, Acting Commissioner; and to the Division of Foreign Labor Conditions of the Bureau which performs such a valuable public service in its research in the field of foreign labor. Dr. Arnold Zempel, Executive Director and his staff in the Office of International Labor Affairs, Department of Labor; and Mr. Joseph Godson, U.S. Labor Attache at the U.S. Embassy in London made valuable suggestions for improving the manuscript. Nor can the assistance be overestimated of Miss Margaret Brickett and her staff in the Department of Labor Library, and the late Laura A. Thompson, whose assiduity, scholarship and foresight made the library the home of an exceptional collection of British labor literature.

To my British friends in the TUC and Labor Party with whom I have had the good fortune to exchange views and discuss the various aspects of British labor problems since the close of World War II, my heartfelt thanks. In this connection I owe much to Mr. Douglas Houghton, M.P., the late Jim Campbell, general secretary of the National Union of Railwaymen and to the other members of the TUC General Council and National Executive of the Labor Party, and the staff members of these organizations who so generously gave of their time and effort in providing material and suggestions for the manuscript. For many personal insights into post-war British labor thought I am indebted to the late Arthur Deakin, the general secretary of the Transport and General Workers Union, who played such a powerful role in the affairs of British labor during the post-war reconstruction period.

Without the devoted assistance and encouragement of my wife this book would not have been completed.

The views and conclusions are the author's and are not a reflection of those who contributed toward their formulation. Nor can they be considered in any way a statement of the views or policies of the Department of State.

HERBERT E. WEINER

Washington, D. C.

CONTENTS

ABOUT THE AUTHOR

A veteran foreign service officer specializing in labor affairs, Herbert E. Weiner has been assistant labor attache in London, labor attache in Australia, and specialist for British Commonwealth affairs in the U.S. Department of Labor. In the Department of State he is concerned with U.S. policy in the International Labor Organization and serves as a member of the American delegation to the ILO.

Mr. Weiner has written previously on British, Australian, Canadian labor affairs as well as on general international labor problems. Articles by him have appeared in the Political Service Quarterly, the Christian Science Monitor and Monthly Labor Review.

He has taught economics and social science at City College in New York and holds M.A. and Ph.D. degrees in economics from Columbia University.

Low's comment on British labor's search for a modernized formula for public ownership.

Nationalization's effect on labor's election prospects as viewed by Low.

A comment on British labor's uncertainty over nationalization.

Three members of the TUC General Council view the return of the one-time pet that refused to disappear.

I

ORIGINS AND EARLY DEVELOPMENT

Until the end of World War I nationalization was not of sufficient importance to capture the center of attention of the British trade union movement, much less that of the nation as a whole. In the half century following the appearance in 1868 of the Trades Union Congress, the trade union movement was concerned mainly with building its independent political and economic power, and adjusting to profound changes in the industrial and legal environment. These years also witnessed the shift of the main body of trade union support from nonpartisan to partisan political action, and the growth of socialistic influences over the policies and leadership of British labor.

Nationalization reflected the general transition of the policies of the trade union movement from what was essentially a Liberal orientation to that of a socialistic orientation. Thus from a concept first accepted by the TUC in the Liberal tradition of seeking to create the conditions for maximum individual economic freedom, nationalization gradually became transformed into a collectivist idea which, on the whole, regarded communal action as preferable to reliance on individual economic interest as a source of benefit to society. In this context nationalization, initially supported by the unions as a land measure to cure depressed farm conditions and to eliminate the restrictive elements in land monopoly during the latter nineteenth century, evolved into a broader measure for the expropriation of other forms of monopoly and eventually into a sectional proposal by labor to eliminate the private owner as the controlling power in industry.

During this period nationalization was little more than a propaganda slogan subordinated, forgotten, or revived in the light of other trade union demands. At most it was a very distant objective. Nevertheless, as a trade union issue it grew steadily in importance and content until under the impact of World War I it was magnified into a national issue—crystallized around the problems of the coal industry—over which the trade unions were carried to the verge of revolutionary activity.

1

THE EARLY TUC AND NATIONALIZATION, 1868-1900

In its early years the TUC was indifferent and even hostile to the idea of social ownership. Radical theorists advocating the reconstruction of society, generally designated as socialists, were not highly regarded by trade unionists. Even the co-operative movement, while considered fraternal, was frequently the subject of bitter reproach by trade union leaders as a result of disputes with cooperative societies over wages and working conditions.

Within the TUC the socialists were a small, though significantly influential, minority. They were attacked as interlopers; and they had to overcome powerful sentiment in the trade unions against establishing ties with any single disciplined political party or set of doctrines. Thus at the 1895 congress the socialists (among them Keir Hardie) were the main targets of a rather successful purge. Four years later a resolution to form the Labor Representation Committee, for which the socialists campaigned vigorously, was passed only narrowly over stiff opposition to the idea of independent labor representation, including that of the powerful coal and cotton unions.[1]

Nevertheless, on the whole, there was a steady rise in the influence of trade unionists with socialist tendencies. Important "new unionist" leaders who had been strongly influenced by the ideas of various socialists such as Sidney Webb, H. M. Hyndman, Eleanor Marx and others, rose to prominence especially with the organization of unskilled labor following the successful 1889 dock strike. The pattern of socialist thought became increasingly attractive to trade unionists. During the depressed 1880's and 1890's the socialists provided the hard-pressed workingman with a sympathetic theoretical explanation of his problems. They cast him in the role of a victim of the inexorable workings of the economic system. They also formulated immediate programs of social and economic reform on which socialists and trade unionists could make common cause. What was more, at the party political level trade union leaders were becoming increasingly estranged from the Liberal Party, where most of them had found an accommodation as the political channel of reform.

When nationalization appeared in the resolutions of the TUC in the 1880's the organization was dominated by leaders and unions oriented towards the Radical wing of the Liberal Party. Though these resolutions in many respects sounded "socialistic," and reflected a potent strain of idealism among trade unionists, they were in accordance with the Liberal-Radical tradition of social reform. Under these circumstances, nationalization resolutions were necessarily of a temper quite acceptable to a substantial range of political and industrial opinion, including that of anti-socialists and some sections of the business community.

Nationalization was associated principally with the problems of anachronistic systems of land tenure and taxation which were regarded as root causes of social and economic injustice. In the main nationalization was based on demands for the conversion of natural monopolies from private to public benefit. Thus, many non-socialist as well as socialist thinkers argued that land values increased automatically with the growth of population and with economic development bringing its owners unearned increment which rightfully belonged to the nation.

The views which Henry George expressed while in Britain in the 1880's as to the relationships between economic distress, industrial progress and the private ownership of land made a distinct impression on British land reformers. But many of them went farther than George. They advocated outright nationalization rather than a single tax that would return the social value of the land to the community. Another comparable and not unrelated influence on the discussions of the land question in Britain was the controversy over home rule and the twin problem of land reform for Ireland which roused strong sympathies among British social reformers and in British labor.

The TUC passed its first nationalization resolution at the 1882 congress. It called for "extensive reforms of the land laws of England, Scotland, and Wales," which were "crippling agricultural industry," and declared that "no reform will be complete short of nationalization of the land."[2] This resolution was rescinded by an overwhelming vote at the next congress amidst charges that it had been passed the previous year only after many of the delegates had gone home. But in the succeeding years the opposition to nationalization resolutions steadily dwindled.

The 1886 congress, during which Henry George was a subject of favorable reference, passed a resolution which coupled the welfare of the worker and his employer in opposition to the landlord. It endorsed the general theme that in the interest of the free functioning of private enterprise the state should take over the property rights of those exercising natural monopolies. The TUC urged nationalization of royalty rents because they were "iniquitous and injurious— iniquitous because they form a monopoly of our mineral resources when they should be used for the good of all; injurious because they place a tax upon our staple industry, interfering with and hindering our commercial prosperity, restricting the profit of the capitalist, and limiting the already too small wages of the workman."[3]

From then on the idea of nationalization did not arouse any significant opposition at annual congresses nor, for that matter, stir any urgent interest either. Resolutions were either forgotten or passed in a routine manner, depending upon the interest of the congress in other topics. Though socialistic influences reached a sort of peak when the 1894 congress placed the TUC on record for the nationalization of "the whole of the means of production, distribution, and exchange,"[4] this stand was repudiated by the following one. While the latter congress rejected the idea of total nationalization, it reaffirmed the demand for the nationalization of land, minerals, and railways,[5] and urged the municipalization of the Port of London to reorganize it to meet the competition of the subsidized Continental ports.

Though socialists continued to grow in influence in the TUC, resolutions on nationalization, usually carried unanimously, were mainly the sort which non-socialists either regarded as harmless or which could gain strong justification on other than doctrinaire socialist grounds. Nationalization as formulated by the TUC was directed primarily at the vestigial privileges of land ownership which had become the symbol of the accrual to the non-producer of unearned increment through the exercise of property rights over the nation's basic natural resources. This "radical" approach to the "land question" had become a badge of progressive thinking and could find a respectable basis in 19th century classical economic theory. As assimilated by British socialists, the justifications for land nationalization were extended to all monopoly which they came to believe was the ultimate natural reward to the entrepreneur who defeats his competitors.

NATIONALIZATION AND LIBERAL REFORM, 1900-1914

In the years between the turn of the century and World War I the trade union movement was concerned principally with the problems of its political and industrial consolidation, and the profound challenge to its legal position resulting from defeats in the courts.

The national economy was in a condition of general prosperity. Yet there was apprehension. Britain was not retaining her share of the rising volume of international trade. Unemployment was low; but real wages fell as retail prices rose and money wages failed to keep pace when they did not actually fall. The unions, though expanding in membership, found it difficult to cope with the economic impact of the reorganization of business into large commercial and industrial combinations, and employers' vigorous anti-union campaigns on the job and in the courts. In particular, the Taff-Vale decisions of 1900-01 had undermined the trade unions' principal industrial weapons—striking and picketing; and the Osborne Judgments of 1908-09 had declared *ultra vires* the use of union funds for political purposes.

On the other hand during the years leading up to World War I trade unions and workingmen could find substantial reason for satisfaction in the area of social and labor legislation. The Liberal government provided for expanded workman's compensation, old age pensions, the establishment of trade boards for sweated industries, a national employment exchange system, and national health and unemployment insurance schemes. Nevertheless the trade unions felt insecure politically. And the flow of circumstances impelled them to throw their support increasingly to the Labor Party with the object of assuring for themselves an ally in Parliament committed to the same general objectives rather than to continue to rely on bargaining with the older parties.

Within the industrial sphere there was an intensified movement towards labor solidarity, too. This took the form of the development of amalgamations and industrial unions and the arrival at agreements among unions for sympathetic action to match the power of the employers in the event of conflict. Two products of these developments were the creation of the first deliberately planned industrial union in 1913, the National Union of Railwaymen, and the formation the next year of the Triple Industrial Alliance made up of the National Union of Railwaymen, Transport Workers' Federation and Miners' Federation.

Nationalization, Liberal and Labor. Compared with other problems, nationalization did not loom large in the labor picture in the first decade of the century. Moreover, on this question as on other more important ones, the Labor Party, Liberal Government, and the main body of the trade union movement had developed a considerable measure of mutual accommodation. Nationalization, accordingly, was defined by the TUC predominantly as a solution to protect the public interest from the abuses of monopoly. More specifically, it was tied to questions of tax and land tenure abuses, the exaction of royalties for mineral rights by land owners, the use of discriminatory freight rates by the railway companies to eliminate effective competition, and monopolistic practices by other large business combinations.

With respect to the nationalization of industrial monopoly the trade unions were governed in much of their thinking by their fears over the widening disparity of bargaining power between the employer and the worker, and the possible threat to organized labor in the industrial and political arena contained in the growth of big business combinations with monopolistic objectives. In this the unions were not too distant from Liberal advocates of nationalization who saw government control or ownership of monopolies as necessary to preserve liberty in the economic sphere in order to head off what they regarded as the threat to political liberty that might follow ultimately from the concentration of economic power.

But for the most part the trade union attitude toward nationalization, as expressed by the TUC, was vague and marked only by mild interest. Nationalization resolutions were either completely absent from congress discussions or merely entered for the record, and their character could be regarded as being quite compatible with a Liberal philosophy.[6] On such issues as the nationalization of railroads, canals, land and mineral royalties the position of the TUC corresponded in large measure to the views expressed by prominent Liberals, as for example, Winston Churchill. Churchill while distinguishing between Liberal reform and socialism called for the nationalization of railways, canals, and other services which were in the nature of monopolies. In one speech made while Undersecretary for Colonies in the Campbell-Bannerman government, Churchill, an ardent advocate of free trade (which the TUC also supported), admonished his audience: "I would recommend you not be scared in discussing any of these proposals because some old woman comes along and tells you they are Socialistic. If you take my advice, you will judge each case on its merits."[7]

Nevertheless, despite the strength of Liberal-Radical traditions, socialistic influences of various stripes grew stronger in trade union thinking and showed themselves in the approach of the TUC to nationalization.[8] This became apparent in the years leading up to World War I in what was probably the most extensive and bitter wave of industrial unrest in British history. There was an atmosphere of intense labor-management antagonism. The trade unions became impatient with the possibilities of political action, and feelings deepened within the trade unions that the government could not be considered neutral, but favored the interests of business over those of the workingman.

Thus the trade unions preferred to turn towards direct industrial action rather than to rely too much on political channels. Together with this militant and somewhat radical mood there was a certain growth of a politicalism, pleasing to Liberals and revolutionary syndicalist and antagonistic to the state socialists, and a renewed emphasis on ideas that workers could protect their interests in industry best by concentrating on control of the job.

With respect to nationalization the corresponding distrust of state power was reflected in skepticism as to the beneficence of the government as an employer. This opened the way for what evolved in succeeding years into proposals for varying versions of "workers control." However, while revolutionary syndicalists insisted on complete workers' ownership as opposed to state ownership of industry, and rejected any proposals which implied a partnership with a capitalist management, the main body of the trade union movement couched its demands in terms of a voice in the decisions made by management in state-owned enterprises.

"Workers Participation." The revolutionary syndicalists made their influence felt within the TUC, although they amounted to little more than a vocal fraction denounced at the annual congresses as disruptors. But there were also other significant currents flowing in the same direction. The skepticism as to the advantages to the worker having the state as an employer, and the demand that employees have a voice in the conduct of industry was strong, especially among the discontented postal unions. In addition, trade unions were steadily being accorded greater participation in the nation's social and economic machinery. Much of this was due to the recognition by the Liberal government of the trade unions' new status in the community. Accordingly, trade unions were given participation in the management of public undertakings in contexts that contradicted syndicalist ideas and ran contrary to the conceptions of many socialists. Thus, the Liberal government in 1908 provided for two labor members on the Port of London authority—a public corporation.[9] And it made concessions to the traditional interest of trade unions in sickness and unemployment benefits by providing for their participation in the administration of the national health and unemployment insurance schemes in 1911.[10] These events set significant concerete precedents for future discussions on "workers' control."

The national insurance scheme established the principle of state operation in a field previously in private hands, and the partnership of organized labor in administering a public service. It also placed the trade unions, which gained great advantages in recruiting members through the operation of the act, in competition with private industrial insurance companies. The 1911 TUC added nationalization of private industrial life insurance to its other nationalization demands.[11] Resolutions for a national insurance scheme to take over all or part of the private life insurance business (especially burial benefits) were passed thenceforth periodically at annual congresses, though not without objections from the agents working for private companies, and expressions of concern for the cooperative insurance societies.

Official TUC policy did not stray very far from gradualist Fabian socialist ideas of state-owned enterprise being managed without special regard for sectional interests, but the idea of workers participating in the management of state undertakings did make headway in trade union policy, if from diverse motivations. Thus the TUC made clear during the formative public discussions of the insurance proposals that "no system of compulsory state insurance for unemployment will be acceptable to the organized workers unless the trade unions shall have adequate representation in the management."[12] This was the first "workers control" resolution the TUC ever passed. However, with respect to nationalized industry generally, the TUC made no defined demand for labor representation on the managing boards. Though there was a revival of interest just before World War I in resolutions for the nationalization of land, minerals, mines, canals, and railways, there were only vague references to "democratic control." Emphasis was on the Fabian concept of achieving industrial democracy through labor representation in the House of Commons. In this vein the last pre-war congress refrained from asking for direct workers' representation on the managements of nationalized industries. But it did declare that "nationalization of public services, such as the Post Office, is not necessarily advantageous to the employees and the working class unless accompanied by steadily increasing democratic control both by the employees and the representatives of the working classes in the House of Commons. It, therefore, pledges itself to work steadily to develop public opinion in both these directions."[13]

Nevertheless, it is of interest to note that the June 1914 conference of the National Union of Railwaymen, formed the previous year under a measure of syndicalist influence, prepared a resolution for that year's trades union congress (which was not held because of the outbreak of war) declaring that "No system of State ownership will be acceptable to organized railwaymen which does not guarantee to them their full political and social rights, allow them a due measure of control and responsibility in the safe and efficient working of the railway system, and assure to them a fair and equitable participation of the increased benefits likely to accrue from a more economical and scientific administration."[14]

To sum up, between the turn of the century and the outbreak of World War I the meaning of nationalization in trade union thought underwent a gradual transition in its purpose and political coloration. It reflected the nation-wide integration of important sectors of the economy, the widening acceptance of intervention by the national government into economic affairs, the waning support in the trade unions for Liberalism and its replacement by collectivist thinking, and the changing status of organized labor in the community. Though still undefined in trade union policy, nationalization no longer reflected the schisms between the business and landed interests. It increasingly took on a meaning for the trade unions as a route for the "liberation of the worker" by changing the employer.

At the same time, while the trade union movement was dominated by Fabian socialist concepts of state-owned industry and the supremacy of community over sectional interests, these concepts were modified by a combination of ingrained Liberal distrust of state power and the rooting of conceptions within organized labor that the worker must take measures to insure the protection of his interests against the state as an employer. The net effect was to develop in the trade union movement a belief that while there should be an extension of government control or ownership of industry, if the worker were to benefit from it he should strive to place the management of government and industry in the hands of those committed to his immediate interests and long term aspirations.

THE IMPACT OF WORLD WAR I

World War I transformed British organized labor into a major independent political and industrial force. The mass influx of semi-skilled and unskilled labor changed the social composition of the trade unions. The accompanying infusion of labor with a spirit of militant radicalism served to complete the conversion of nationalization in trade union policy from a Liberal to a socialistic conception.

Under wartime conditions the influence of organized labor vastly expanded and coalesced as membership multiplied and military need placed a high strategic value on labor's political and economic co-

operation. British labor's new power compelled general respect, and
its participation in national affairs beyond the limits of what had previously been accepted as its area of interest came to be taken for
granted. Hand in hand with this growth of influence went increased
independent activity at home and abroad, the collection of issues to
make up a practicable and wide-ranged collectivist labor program,
and an intensified belief that the workingman could and should or-
ganize to influence the course of national policy.

Nationalization rose to the prominence of a major demand which
became significant to organized labor as a measure to win early industrial reform as well as to alter the organization of society. With
socialistic elements dominant in British organized labor, nationalization was transformed into a political and industrial objective through
which the labor movement hoped to eliminate industrial exploitation,
satisfy the revolutionary spirit, and initiate a new social order for
which many thought the time was at hand.

The relationship of nationalization to ideas for socializing natural
monopolies in order to liberalize the economy faded rapidly. Instead,
nationalization, as advocated by the trade unions, moved into another
frame of reference which Liberals could not accept. To that extent,
nationalization as an aspect of collectivism emerged from the war
more sharply defined as a general issue to divide British political
parties and sections of the economic community.

Reorientation of the Labor Outlook. Wartime experience served
to impregnate organized labor's conception of nationalization with a
fundamental conviction as to the superiority of the centralized state
control of industry and the right of the workingman to some sort of
partnership in the management of industry in view of the special direct stake he had in its operation.

The broad lines of argument made for nationalization during the
wartime trades union congresses were as follows: The war had
proven that the economy was capable of producing far more than it
had in the past; the need to resort to the government control of vital
industries during the war was a supreme test which had demonstrated
the comparative inadequacy of private competitive enterprise; and if
continued in peacetime, the government operation or control of industry would give workers a higher standard of living and a fairer
distribution of the national product. Implicit in this was the assumption that there could be carried over into the running of nationalized
industries in peacetime the social and national spirit generated in
wartime.

At annual congresses these arguments were increasingly supplemented on the ideological level by assertions along the following lines: Business competition was anarchic, self-defeating and inefficient. The growth of business combinations and the centralized planning of production during the war were evidence of both the natural tendencies towards "trustification" in the economic structure and the benefits that would flow from planning. Therefore, nationalization would not only expropriate the power of private monopoly in the public interest, but eliminate wasteful competition as well. Moreover, it was claimed, nationalization would extend the democratic process and social conscience into industry, take private profit out of war, stabilize the economy, and lead to a general improvement in the standard of living and the condition of the workingman. And finally nationalization was seen as the ultimate instrument for intercepting the flow of wealth before it reached private pockets, in order to assure its just distribution for the national good.

The trends favoring and shaping nationalization that had appeared in the pre-war period were intensified during the war. Successive wartime congresses reflected the increased politicalization of industrial problems, a growth of radical revolutionary activism among rank and file unionists, the greater stress the trade unions' placed on their kinship with the Labor Party and the Cooperative Movement, and the fading away among trade union leaders of any substantial opposition to collectivist ideas. The wartime experience especially strengthened labor's sectional outlook and made the trade unions more determined than ever to enhance their status and participation in public affairs and industry—a feeling which made the doctrines of guild socialism, for example, in a measure appealing to those who could not accept the revolutionary aspects of syndicalism. As expressions of "workers' control" these ideas impressed themselves particularly on the programs of the postal, railway, and other transport, and mining unions.

Though the trade union movement as a whole from beginning to end threw its support behind the war effort, nevertheless, as the war progressed disillusion set in and the anti-war traditions within British labor became more influential in shaping its view of the world. Grievances against business, the government, and the older political parties mounted and took root in labor thinking. Restiveness in the trade union movement spread with war-weariness, the spiralling cost of living, war profiteering, and attempts by employers to eliminate permanently the safeguards unions had given up for the duration of the war. The state, a dominant factor in the wartime economy, became a major participant in labor affairs with its own vested interests. Often the state was a principal contestant against the trade unions in disputes, and this provided opportunities for them to taste victory occasionally over the government by the use of their industrial power. Also the convergence of interests on war issues in common opposition to the policies of the Liberal-led government drew the Trades Union Congress, the Cooperative Union, and the Labor Party, closer together and brought into sight the formation of a "triune of labor" concerned with the problems of the workingman as an employee, consumer, and citizen.

Political discontent in the domestic field, which by the end of the war led organized labor, through the Labor Party, to set forth on an independent course in presenting itself to the electorate, was supplemented by developments in the international arena. The wave of revolution on the Continent that began in 1917 roused a sense of historic urgency among British labor leaders who had become convinced that the worker had a special role to play on the world stage. There were strong feelings in British labor that the professed democratic aims of the war had been betrayed for ulterior national ambitions, that an international clique was conspiring to thwart the popular will and preserve established privilege in the respective countries after the war, and that private business had reaped inordinate gains from wartime tragedy. By the end of the war the mood in the British labor movement was dominated by a belief that the workingman deserved a reward for his sacrifices, and that he was not likely to obtain it or any significant improvement in his condition without using his collective strength. With respect to the trade unions, having shown the value of their participation in the war effort, they were determined not to have their independent influence discounted after the war.

The Wartime Congresses. At the successive wartime congresses, the themes emphasized by the resolutions on nationalization were: the gains in efficiency that could be made by the government reorganization and operation of industry, opposition to the return to private control of enterprises taken over by the government during the war, the common interest of the worker and consumer in opposition to the businessman, and the importance of granting to workers participation in the management of nationalized industries in accord with their enhanced status in the comunity.

At the first wartime congress in 1915, the TUC, in a resolution moved by the railway unions, announced its opposition to the return to private control of the railways after the war. It urged also that an advisory committee to the management of the nationalized railways be established on which railway employees would have elected representatives.[15] At the same congress the sentiments of the railwaymen for a voice in management were restated more strongly by the spokesmen for the postal workers. Speaking for a resolution urging "the democratic control" of the public services, a delegate from the Postman's Federation admonished: "Whatever advantages we have been able to secure for the postal workers have been wrested from the State; they have never been voluntarily conceded. That is an important point, which should never be lost sight of in our efforts towards the extension of the nationalization principle; and in order to safeguard the position of workers, there should be a steady demand for democratic control in respect of all the public services taken over by the State."[16]

The next year the TUC declared as its general policy, "that the future efforts of trade unionism should be focussed on the attainment of the increased nationalization of industry, accompanied by increased democratic control."[17] Also for the first time since the founding of the TUC, the Parliamentary Committee presented to a congress for ratification a declaration of basic outlook and objectives which summarized the agreed thinking that had evolved in the trade union movement on significant social and economic problems over the years, and especially as a result of wartime experience. With respect to the organization of industry, while providing predominantly for the continuance of private enterprise, the manifesto called for the government control or ownership of important sections of the wartime economy and the nationalization of all railways, waterways, and mines on a permanent basis.[18] The same congress also demanded that on a nationalized railway system it should be arranged "for the trade unions concerned to have such a share in the management . . . as will enable railway workers to have a real voice in the control of conditions in their life and work.[19]

By 1917 the TUC, in addition to its more or less traditional demands, endorsed resolutions which called for nationalization as the method of dealing with problems relating to temperance, the rehabilitation of canals and waterways, food production, food profiteering and land speculation. The congress also reaffirmed its support of the postal unions' demand for the democratic control of the public services.[20]

The "Jubilee Congress," which took place two months before the Armistice, called for the nationalization of electric power supply, land, the supply and distribution of milk, life insurance[21] and the co-ordination under public ownership or control of all principal means of transport and communications—railways, canals, road transport, postal, telegraph and aerial services.[22] For the first time at a trades union congress a resolution for the nationalization of mining carried the imprint of "workers' control" when it declared, "that the mines and minerals of the country should be owned and democratically controlled by the State."[23]

"Labor and the New Social Order."   In the political sphere the Labor Party on February 26, 1918, adopted a socialist objective. This was part of its preparation for presenting itself to the voters as an "unfettered political party."   The Labor Party also summarized and incorporated the nationalization policies of the trade union movement as part of its own program for postwar reconstruction.[24]   In doing so, the Labor Party had to consider the many practicalities of giving political expression to the grievances of the workingman while avoiding the appearance of championing a narrow sectional interest.

The Labor Party justified nationalization along the same lines as the trade union movement.   It claimed that government ownership or control of industry had proved its superiority to private enterprise under the stress of war and therefore even greater benefits could be derived if the opportunity were seized to continue to implement this principle in peace time.   The program of British organized labor and the place of nationalization in postwar reconstruction were set forth in "Labor and the New Social Order" and offered for the consideration of the electorate in December, 1918.[25]

The program submitted by the National Executive Committee to the Seventeenth Labor Party Conference in January 1918 for ratification committed the party to the reorganization of society with nationalization chosen as the instrument to perform key functions.   It was drafted by Sidney Webb, at the time the Fabian Society representative on the National Executive Committee.   The program called for the creation of a new social order based "on a deliberately planned cooperation in production and distribution for the benfit of all who participate by hand or by brain.[26]   Declaring that World War I marked the end of a civilization, it announced that "The individualist system of capitalist production, based on the private ownership and competitive administration of land and capital, with its reckless 'profiteering' and wage slavery . . . may, we hope, indeed, have received a death blow."[27]

The program offered a "systematic and comprehensive plan" for post-war reconstruction, as an alternative to that of the government. It included a wide range of proposals for social and labor legislation; demobilization and anticipated post-war unemployment; educational, electoral and fiscal reform (including a denunciation of taxation of cooperative dividends); foreign and colonial policy; international trade; and the public ownership and control of industry.

The Four Pillars of the House that the Labor Party proposed to erect "resting on the common foundation of the Democratic control of society in all its activities" were termed:

"The Universal Enforcement of the National Minimum"

"The Democratic Control of Industry"

"The Revolution in National Finance; and"

"The Surplus Wealth for the Common Good."[28]

The proposals for nationalization enumerated and extended those which had evolved at trade union congresses and Labor Party conferences. The principle of the common ownership of land was to be implemented at suitable opportunities. Railways and mines, (already under wartime government operation) and electric power supply (for which plans of reorganization by the national government were under consideration) were recommended for immediate nationalization. Railways, canals, harbors, roads, steamship lines, and posts and telegraphs were to be united into a national service of communication and transport. Combining elements of communal socialism, "workers' control," and the supremacy of national over local authority, the program declared that these industries were "to be worked, unhampered by capitalists, private or purely local interests (and with a steadily increasing participation of the organized workers in the management both central and local) exclusively for the common good."[29]

In addition to the nationalization of the great industrial undertakings, the Labor Party proposed the expropriation of private industrial and life insurance companies "to secure a clear field for the beneficent work of the friendly [i.e., the mutual] societies," and the development of public health insurance administered by a government department. Provision would be made for universal coverage at cheaper rates, the protection of policy holders against the effects of the depreciation of securities held by insurance funds and the suspension of workers' war bonuses, and for civil service status for insurance agents concerned with the loss of their jobs.

To obtain temperance reform, the program recommended that the control over the manufacture and the retailing of liquor be taken out of the hands of those profiting from the promotion of its sale and transferred to the control of localities. The localities would have the right to prohibit or license the manufacture and sale of liquor, or operate the liquor business as a public enterprise. In the area of "municipal socialism," the program suggested that municipalities should not rest content with acquiring control over local water, gas, electricity, and transport systems, but that they should extend their ownership of the land as required for such enterprises as public housing, town planning and general welfare activities, and take over such common services as the retailing of household coal and milk, where not already organized by cooperative societies.

As a general principle, "Labor and the New Social Order" declared that other main industries should be nationalized as the opportunity offers, especially those industries becoming monopolies.

Though the Labor Party program was socialistic, it nevertheless left the way open for support that extended over the spectrum of socialists, trade unionists, cooperators, sympathetic reformers and others who at the end of the war were ready to break with traditional habits of thought. Thus the Labor Party conference rebuffed a delegate from the doctrinaire Marxist-oriented British Socialist Party (a socialist affiliate of the Labor Party). He had sharply attacked the Labor Party's intention of working towards the new social order by the "deliberately planned cooperation in production and distribution," as an attempt at compromise with capitalism. He had demanded instead a forthright declaration for the "social democratic ownership and control of industry." Sidney Webb replied to the critic: "It was true that in the Constitution they had it down that the party was working for the common ownership of the means of production, etc., . . . but they did not want repeatedly, over and over again, to ring the changes on the old shibboleths. The resolutions [ratifying "Labor and the New Social Order"] were not an appeal to the converted but the basis of an appeal to the 20 million electors—10 or 12 million of them being new electors. The British Socialist Party had talked for many years, but its programs had not been commensurate with its energy or persistence."[30]

IN SUMMARY

Nationalization by the end of World War I derived importance as a key feature of a distinctive, if embryonic, labor program in the company of issues ranging over a wide field of domestic and foreign policy. Nationalization showed the impression on labor thinking of the shifts in authority and responsibility from a local to a national level, the development of political consciousness in the trade unions, and the inclination of the trade unions to look more and more to political solutions to resolve economic problems. Nationalization reflected the rise in the belief of the trade union movement in its own strength, and the decline in its previous neutrality towards the economic system and the major political parties.

As an objective, nationalization became a connecting link among organizations of labor reform in Britain and an expression of British labor's sympathy with the aspirations of workingmen's organizations in other countries. Nationalization was still primarily propagandistic in appeal, vague in concept, and undetailed in its plan of application. Nevertheless the war placed the nationalization of some important industries within the realm of realization for the first time. As defined by the TUC, nationalization showed the influence of doctrines, such as guild socialism, which emphasized the special interests of labor, and to which the fluidity and disillusionment of the times made organized labor increasingly receptive. But in its fundamentals nationalization remained an expression of British non-doctrinaire communal socialism to be applied in terms of given situations. In these circumstances, the advocates of nationalization were faced with questions of the mutual modifications of interest among the cooperative, political and trade union members of the collectivist alliance, and the balancing of ultimate objectives against immediate goals.

II

TRADE UNION MILITANCY

With the close of World War I nationalization emerged as a national issue of major proportions. Specifically, it became uniquely identified as a technique of trade union-socialist policy, and more broadly with the aspirations of organized labor. The first seven and a half years after the war proved to be an initial and militant phase of a period extending over a quarter of a century during which the British trade union movement worked out its policies for dealing with Britain's long range economic and social problems. During this period the form, method and philosophy of nationalization as a labor concept was moulded by the experiences of industrial and political labor during the post-World War I boom, the long inter-war depression, and World War II.

From the end of the war until the 1926 National Strike nationalization was cast in a setting in which militant radicalism and a belief in the strength of united industrial action reached a high point in British trade union thinking. On the other hand the business community and non-labor political elements were reluctant to recognize the new power of organized labor and were oriented in their economic thinking towards a "return to normalcy." These differences served to complicate the difficulties in the economy which stemmed from the heavy cost to Britain of World War I as well as the more profound changes in world trading patterns. In the subsequent polarization of opinion over the approach to economic and social problems nationalization emerged as an issue for national debate and alignment.

In this context the cleavage which developed over the problems of the coal industry between the trade union movement on the one hand and the employers and the government on the other, and which led eventually to the National Strike, involved a fundamental issue as to the nature of the government's responsibility for the maintenance of the nation's economic health. With respect to the philosophy of British trade unionism the dramatic crystallization of developments in the National Strike laid to rest ideas about the use of industrial militancy to force the hand of the government. Insofar as the strike had a bearing on nationalization as a principle, it established that the nationalization of an industry would have to be obtained by the trade union movement solely by influencing parliamentary action within a broad policy of political and industrial compromise and collaboration.

Though policies of industrial militancy fell into disrepute in the trade union movement after the National Strike, nationalization remained a very real issue. Its importance in public discussion grew with the continuance of the depression, the aggravation of Britain's economic problems, the embitterment of industrial relations, and the clash between traditional and challenging economic ideas. What was more, nationalization in increasing measure roused strong emotions rooted in broader controversies over the eradication of human exploitation, the more equal distribution of income and economic opportunity, and the reorganization and development of given industries on which the well-being of large sections of the working population depended.

NATIONALIZATION AS A SOCIALIST-UNION POLICY

In the years between the Armstice and the 1926 strike, nationalization, as defined by the trade union movement, reflected the changing political and economic environment. Nationalization became symbolic of the decline in individualistic thinking and the completion of the transition of the trade unions towards acceptance of socialistic collectivism as their orthodox orientation. Nationalization became an issue which drew the trade unions closer to the Labor Party and widened their differences with the older parties. Its formulation became part of the general development in the trade unions of industrial and economic policies concerned with unemployment, fiscal problems, and the whole question of government participation in economic life. This was in keeping with the beginnings in the trade unions of an approach for systematically working out interrelated policies on all major national economic and political problems.

The trade union attitude towards nationalization after World War I bore little resemblance to that of five years before. It was colored by the disappointments and economic hardship that followed the military victory. The belief was strong that an opportunity for the reorganization of society had been made possible by the destruction of old institutions during the war. Moreover, among the trade unions there was a decided loss of confidence in an economy dominated by principles of business enterprise.

At trades union congresses nationalization became a term that stirred emotions and vigorous debate. Advocates of nationalization denied the theory that had dominated the economic outlook of the TUC since its founding—namely that, in the main, the operation and allocation of productive resources were best left to private enterprise. They emphasized the anti-social aspects of private business, implied that there was something unethical about private profit, and declared that government enterprise was more in the community interest than was private enterprise. They saw nationalization as a medium for establishing a higher status for the worker in industry as well as for the sweeping extension of economic and social democracy. For these purposes nationalization became an instrument for planning and controlling the economy and sharing the national wealth.

In accordance with previous trends, the steady growth of the socialistic conception of nationalization in the trade unions continued. This had been so in the early part of the century when Britain's trading difficulties largely had been masked by the continuance of earnings from foreign investments and the general rise in the level of international trade. But after the war, as the decline in the world competitive position of the British economy became more pronounced and its effects became visibly widespread, trade unionists and socialists found an even broader and firmer basis of common belief and action.

The economic dislocation of entire industries such as coal, textiles and the metal trades, and the consequent appearance of chronic unemployment on a large scale undermined the belief, in and out of the labor movement, that private enterprise had the resources to cope with these problems or that an economic system based on private incentive contained within it the strength necessary to reorganize the industrial structure. These developments helped to open the way for the general acceptance of government intervention in the economy in ever-widening spheres. In all, it can be said, that while the forces of private enterprise and individualism progressively weakened, those of organized labor and collectivism grew. Moreover, the impact of the Russian Revolution, which was regarded in the thinking of British labor as evidence of the possibility of workers establishing a socialist state, served to radicalize further the labor view of society.

MILITANCY, NATIONALIZATION AND COAL PROBLEMS

After World War I the Labor Party replaced the Liberal Party as the second national party. By 1924 Labor was in charge of a minority government. Despite this political success, limited as it was, the trade union movement continued to be driven by the spirit of industrial militancy which had made itself felt before 1914 and which had grown enormously during the war. There were strong feelings in the trade union movement that the power of the government must be brought to bear on behalf of the working man and could not be regarded as neutral on questions of economic interest; that organized labor must receive recognition and participation in the operation of industry commensurate with its special stake in it; and that "indirect" party political action was not as effective as "direct action" in impressing on the government the trade unions' point of view. Accordingly, while trade union and electoral support for the Labor Party grew, the conviction was reinforced in the trade unions that the real and reliable strength of organized labor lay in its industrial rather than political force—something which was reflected in the reorganization of the TUC, and in other manifestations to centralize and coordinate the strength of the trade unions as an instrument of labor power in the community.

With respect to nationalization, the main demands of the trade unions at the time of the Armistice were for the retention by the government of the ownership and control of those industries it had acquired during the war—especially railways and coal. There was in support of this a current of public opinion that the government should continue to hold a dominating position in the economy in order to switch the resources of the country to new major peaceful purposes of social and economic reconstruction. In addition to munitions manufacture, the war had provided examples of the use of governmental authority to establish and operate basically civilian industry (e.g. beet sugar and dyes), and to promote operational efficiency, as in the unification of the railway systems. Moreover, wartime experience had shown that technological developments may give rise not only to undertakings of commercial value, but also to those which require large amounts of government financial assistance, or uniquely involve public policy or the national economic or military interest.

In subsequent years in empirical fashion these aforementioned considerations entered into the decisions by non-labor governments to establish the partial government ownership and subsidization of aerial services, to create a Forestry Commission (a public corporation) to implement a national afforestation program by planting state forests or cultivating others in cooperation with private owners, to reorganize the national electricity supply under the Central Electricity

Board (a public corporation), and to set up radio broadcasting as a government-owned public service under the British Broadcasting Corporation.

However, immediately after the cessation of hostilities, while the government of Prime Minister David Lloyd George in certain circumstances was willing to continue a measure of public ownership in partnership with private industry,[1] the tide of opinion favored its policy of eliminating wartime controls and returning industry, insofar as was practicable, to private operation. Wartime controls had developed largely as a series of improvisations to meet emergencies and there was little challenge to the assumption that their justification had ended with the war.[2] This, notwithstanding the protests of organized labor and others who saw an opportunity being missed to reorganize industry with increased efficiency and with a concept of social consciousness.

After the war proposals for the integration and nationalization of electric power were rejected. Government-owned factories were returned or sold to private owners. The railways, nearly all of which were amalgamated during the war into four large non-competitive systems, were returned to four new companies in August 1921, notwithstanding promises by the government during the 1918 general election to nationalize them.[3] The coal industry, too, was returned to private control in March 1921 over the bitter protests of the Miners' Federation; but unlike the other cases this one became the test issue between organized labor and the government.

In the post-war years the TUC at one time or another, declared for the public ownership of banking, transport and communications, land, mines and minerals, housing, liquor, and abattoirs. It also went on record as favoring "workers' control" in the form of worker participation in management. At the 1924 congress, nationalization, which had been the subject of resolutions for forty years, was incorporated for the first time into the TUC Standing Orders as part of an Industrial Workers' Charter.

The charter was drawn up as a program of long range economic and social objectives to be sought by the trade union movement. The TUC, accordingly, pledged itself as part of its basic policy to the nationalization of land, mines, minerals, and railways; the extension of state and municipal enterprise for the provision of social necessities and services; and the "proper provision for the adequate participation of the workers in control and management."[4] But no forceful case was made to press these demands—except for coal. The nationaliza-

tion of the coal industry which became an issue of far-reaching political and industrial significance at the end of World War I was not
resolved for the next quarter of a century. Between 1919 and 1926
it became symbolic of the efforts of the trade union movement to
reorganize industry in a manner which would lead to an improvement
in the condition of the working man.

"The Coal Question." With the close of the war, for the first time
in British industrial history, nationalization became an issue of collective bargaining. In a broad sense this reflected the revolutionary feelings seeded in the trade unions prior to the war, and the companion
tendency to threaten the government with industrial action on political issues, e.g. by threatening industrial action in 1919-1920 to pressure the British government to give up its policy of intervention
against the Russian Bolshevik regime.[5] In coal, which was still under
wartime government control, these militant tendencies came to the
surface in connection with a list of demands made by the Miners'
Federation in February 1919. The miners, who were then in a strong
bargaining position, demanded a general wage rise of approximately
30%, a reduction in coal prices and, most controversial of all, the nationalization of the industry along with "workers' control." By the
end of February 1919, in an atmosphere charged with industrial restiveness, and with the railwaymen and transport workers supporting
the miners, it looked as if the Triple Industrial Alliance was on the
verge of demonstrating its solidarity behind a general coal strike.

In these circumstances, the government tentatively offered the miners what amounted to a 10% wage rise to offset the rise in the cost
of living. It offered also to established a statutory commission with
wide powers of recommendation on the miners' demands and the condition of the industry. Alternatively the government threatened to use
its war powers to suppress any strike. Following the strenuous efforts
of its leaders, the Miners' Federation agreed to postpone its strike for
three weeks pending an interim report by the commission of inquiry.

The Sankey Commission. The government named Sir John Sankey,
Justice of the High Court, as chairman of the commission. It appointed six members nominated or approved by the Miners' Federation, three by the mine owners, and three other industry members.
The commission began its work March 3 and presented its reports
March 20, 1919. Of the three reports that came out of the first stage
of the hearings the government accepted that of the chairman and
three independent industry members of the commission. The report
recommended immediate wage rises of approximately 20%, reduc-

tions in hours for underground workers to seven per shift, and the immediate investigation of the question of reorganizing the industry by
nationalization or other methods. With respect to the last, the report
declared: "Even upon the evidence already given the present system
of ownership and working in the coal industry stands condemned and
some other system must be substituted for it, either nationalization
or a method of national purchase and/or joint control."[6]

The Miners' Federation after a ballot of its membership called off
the threatened strike in consideration of the proposed inquiry. The
government promised to implement the recommendations of the second stage hearings of the commission.

The four different reports[7] that in June 1919 came out of the second
stage of the Sankey commission all agreed on the nationalization of
mineral rights and royalties, the reorganization of the retail distribution of coal, and an extension of joint labor-management machinery.
However, the commission was split on the question of the ownership
and operation of the mines. Taken together, Justice Sankey and the
labor members of the commission (a total of seven) recommended
complete nationalization, to which the remaining six industry members of the commission were opposed.

The government adopted as final the wages and hours recommendations of the Sankey commission and in July, 1919, passed the Coal
Mines Regulation (Seven Hours) Act. In August 1919, Prime Minister Lloyd George proposed a plan to nationalize mining royalty rights
as a device to unify the industry, to undertake various measures for
the general rehabilitation of the industry and to improve working conditions, and to give miners a consultative voice in the industry's affairs. But he refused to nationalize the industry itself. In response
to the trade unions' demand that he fulfill the government's promise
to implement the majority view, Lloyd George took the position that
there had been no single majority report. Of the commission, he
claimed, only Justice Sankey and the three independent industry
members had had an open mind, and had not been previously committed on nationalization one way or another. Of these four, three
had recommended against nationalization.[8] The mine owners and
the Miners' Federation rejected the government plan, and it became
a dead letter.

The Path to the National Strike. Thereafter the TUC, in a series of
notable debates extending over the regular congress of September 1919
and two special congresses in December 1919 and March 1920 defeated moves to back the Miners' Federation with a general strike to

force nationalization of the mines. The September congress authorized renewed representations by the TUC to the government in support of the miners' demand for implementation of the Sankey report. The December congress sidetracked the possibility of strike action by deciding on an intense "Mines for the Nation" propaganda campaign jointly with the Labor Party and Miners' Federation in anticipation of the opening of Parliament in February. The campaign failed to rouse the public or parliamentary support hoped for to force the government's hand. The March congress by 3,870,000 to 1,050,000 rejected the miners' motion for a general strike and then voted for a continuance of "political action in the form of intensive political propaganda for a general election."* This in effect put the issue on an indefinite basis as far as the TUC was concerned.

Though the government, still in control of the mines, made some wage concessions to the Miners' Federation in November 1920 following a strike, the collapse of the postwar boom soon undercut the federation's bargaining position. The export price of coal fell in the face of the resurgence of foreign competition, including the heavy German coal reparations. The government returned the mines to private control on March 31, 1921 some four and a half months earlier than originally scheduled. This terminated the agreement reached after the 1920 strike and signalled a three month's strike which for the miners resulted in wage cuts and the elimination of nationwide bargaining. This defeat was embittered by the collapse of the Triple Industrial Alliance in its first test when on "Black Friday," April 15, 1921 it backed down on its original threat to strike in support of the miners.

Despite the events of 1919-1921, in the years that followed there persisted in the trade union movement the tendencies towards the centralization of authority, the faith in the formidability of combined labor action, and the strong sentiment that the trade union movement must demonstrate its solidarity with the miners. Moreover, there was a powerful motivation in the belief that the future of the trade union movement and the economic condition of workingmen in Britain were intimately tied to the resolution of the problems of the declining coal industry. The coal industry became symbolic of Britain's postwar economic problems. With the exception of agriculture, it employed more labor than any other industry. It provided about 10 percent in value of British exports and the bulk of the nation's commercial cargo. And it was the foundation of Britain's industrial life.

From the Armistice onward, with intervals of truce, the industry was characterized by successive labor-management crises: in 1919,

1920, 1921, 1924, 1925, and finally 1926. Compared with a peak in 1913 of 287 million tons mined and 94 million tons exported, British coal output in 1921 fell to a low of 162 million tons,[10] of which 36 million tons were exported. Yet the number of men on the colliery books in 1921 was 1,132,000 compared with 1,107,000 in 1913. Largely because of the stoppage of production of coal in the Ruhr owing to the French occupation, total British output for 1923 recovered to 276 million tons of which 98 million tons were exported. But production and exports fell again in 1925 to 243 million tons and 67 million tons respectively.[11]

Government policy became a vital factor affecting the condition of the industry whether directly in the form of subsidies, as in 1921 and 1925, to tide the industry over critical labor disputes, or through the deflationary effects of the decision to return to the gold standard in 1925, which adversely affected Britain's coal export position. By 1925, almost three-fourths of Britain's tonnage was being produced at a loss.[12] With wage rates and miners' earnings declining, and aggravated by heavy unemployment and underemployment, from the miners' point of view the only hope for the industry lay in the most radical treatment on a national scale—namely, by nationalization.

The trade union movement made the case for coal nationalization a matter of common interest and aligned itself with the Miners' Federation against the coal owners and successive governments whose prevailing policies assumed that the industry could be restored to health under private enterprise.[13] The formation of the first Labor Government in 1924 was to no avail in this respect. Being a minority government dependent on Liberal Party support it was in no position to get a coal nationalization measure through Parliament. Tension in the industry increased with each crisis until on July 31, 1925 ("Red Friday"), the TUC, in supporting the miners' demands against wage reductions, an extension of the working day and in effect a return to district from national bargaining (which the Miners' Federation had regained in 1924), found itself mobilizing to support a threatened general coal strike. During the negotiations leading up to the crisis Prime Minister Stanley Baldwin informed the TUC that he opposed nationalization of the industry because he was convinced that it would not even be as efficient as the existing system.[14]

The Samuel Commission. The strike was averted at the last moment when the government acceded to the unions' demand that it deal directly with the dispute as a responsible party because of the impact of its policies on the industry. After initially resisting the idea the government intervened to subsidize the maintenance of existing wage rates for nine months pending a new investigation by a royal commission. Headed by Sir Herbert Samuel, a Liberal, a commission was appointed to inquire into the issues in the immediate dispute and the problems of the reorganization of the industry, and make recommendations concerning both.

Before the commission, the mine owners proposed a lengthening of hours and reduction in wage rates as the only practical course, while maintaining that little could be done to improve the organization of the industry.[15] The mine owners could prove that with the wartime loss of markets threatening to be permanent, and that with rising costs of transport (which they asked to have reduced) the industry was not paying its way. Nationalization, they contended, was a political and ideological issue, in support of which the Miners' Federation was determined to block the reconstruction of the industry under private enterprise.

The miners' reply was that the real trouble was the wastefulness of piecemeal ownership, the struggle of small mines, and the selfishness of the big rich ones. The miners' spokesmen in their presentation to the commission concentrated on the reorganization of the industry. They insisted on nationalization and rejected any concessions on wages and hours. Their demand was for nationalization—or pending that, such a pooling of mines as would, by throwing the returns of rich mines into the common stock, enable the poorer ones to keep up the wage level.

The commission issued its report March 10, 1926. It did not recommend the nationalization of the mines or any drastic interference with private control. But it did propose the nationalization of mineral-producing land, the reorganization of domestic and export marketing, the organization of research for the efficient production and the extraction of power from coal, the use of the state's land-leasing power to encourage colliery amalgamations to improve efficiency, and the use of compulsory powers where voluntary solutions failed under existing leases. The commission also recommended the continuance of the statutory seven hour day, the extension of joint consultation at the pit level, various amenities, and the introduction of profit-sharing. It condemned the continuance of a coal subsidy as indefensible. The commission concluded unanimously that the condition of the industry could not be attributed to the unrest or restrictions of output among the miners as some of the operators claimed, nor to inefficiency in the management of the mines as the miners claimed.

It was the result of powerful economic forces and had to be met by a fundamental reorganization of the industry involving changes in ownership, management, and relations with other industries.

The government, though not in accord with all the recommendations, agreed on March 24 to accept the Samuel Report—including the nationalization of royalties, and workers' shares in the operation and fortunes of the industry—if the miners and owners did so, too. The negotiations between the owners and the miners, however, proved fruitless. In mid-April 1926 the mine owners posted notices terminating the national agreement and listing their new reduced wage schedule to take effect with the expiration of the subsidy on April 30. For its part the Miners' Federation in a conference decision had committed itself earlier to oppose any lengthening of hours, wage reductions, or return to district agreements.

The situation was deadlocked. The Miners' Federation called on the TUC General Council to implement its pledges of support. It alleged that the miners' dispute was only the first phase in a general onslaught by employers on wages and hours and that the fate of other industries depended on a solution to the coal industry's problems. The TUC, like the Miners' Federation, rejected the Samuel commission's recommendations as inadequate to settle the immediate dispute. The TUC called for "drastic reorganization" of the industry. "In our view," it declared, "the wages and conditions of the mine workers are already so depressed as to render it imperative to seek for other than a further degradation in their standards of life, or the abrogation of present standard hours."[16]

On May Day 1926 the mines were closed. The National Strike (strictly speaking the strike did not become general since it was not carried beyond the first stage) followed on May 3, after last-minute efforts to avert it had failed. The emphasis by the TUC on the industrial aspects of the dispute and its repudiation of any implications that it was challenging the authority of the government were to no avail. The government could not let it appear that a general strike was an irresistible weapon. Nine days later the TUC called off the National Strike, amidst acrimonious exchanges with the miners who stayed out for five months before yielding to sharp wage reductions, the suspension of the statutory seven hour day, and a return to district bargaining.

As for nationalization, the government withdrew its undertaking to implement the Samuel commission's proposals. Prime Minister Baldwin claimed that under existent conditions the government could not create a new financial burden that would be incurred by the purchase of royalties and the creation of a new staff of government officials. However, the government did enact the Mining Industry Act of 1926 which was to facilitate the voluntary amalgamation of mines into sounder economic units. Sir Herbert Samuel referred to it as a "useful little act," and observed that little use was being made of it. He discounted the reasons given by the government for not nationalizing royalties and suggested instead that the real reason was that the Prime Minister's Conservative supporters in Parliament did not want royalty nationalization.[17]

As for the trade union movement, the defeat in 1926 resulted in internal dissension, bitterness, and legislative restrictions (under the Trade Disputes and Trade Unions Act of 1927) which it sought to have undone for the next twenty years. Though the trade unions remained aware of their power, they had learned by hard experience the dangers and responsibilities as well as the advantages of combining their strength to win their objectives by industrial force.

IN SUMMARY

The net effect of the events of the post-war reconstruction period with respect to nationalization may be summed up this way. The dramatic controversies especially in the coal industry, educated and stimulated the general public, employers, the government, and the trade unions into thinking about the implications of nationalization. The integration of British business and trade union organization on a national scale, the imbalance of the British economy, the depressed state of industrial sectors essential to national prosperity favored the intervention of the national government in economic affairs. The differences between liberal-individualistic and labor-collectivist conceptions of nationalization were delineated. Though the idea of nationalization was not a monopoly of collectivists, as a principle it became associated particularly with socialism, and in partisan politics with the Labor Party.

For the trade union movement, in the light of the 1926 strike, nationalization, whatever its industrial significance, became a demand which would have to be dealt with as a political issue and subject to the compromises this implied. This meant that the trade unions would have to modify substantially the pursuit of their special interests if they were to convince the electorate that the nationalization of an industry was in the national interest. It would also be necessary for the trade union movement to become more concrete in evaluating nationalization in terms of its purposes, scope and priority, and with respect to the concessions the trade unions should be prepared to make in bargaining with its allies as well as opponents. All this would serve to dilute the doctrinaire element in nationalization, and keep it subsidiary to issues, such as wages and hours, accepted in and out of the labor movement as primary to trade unionism. However, to the extent that the public ownership or control of some types of economic activity in the national interest won support from many who otherwise might be opposed to socialistic ideas, nationalization would become more of a practical possibility.

III

POLICIES OF PUBLIC OWNERSHIP
AND THE "CONDITION OF BRITAIN"

Between 1926 and the end of World War II the policies and programs of British trade unionism evolved in an environment in which there was a growing disposition towards collectivized action, centralization, and planning. There was a failing belief in the natural harmony of a society based on economic individualism. This was reflected in a turning away from the traditions of the free market in favor of the modification of competition. All of Britain's major political parties became increasingly committed to state action, though with differences as to degree and emphasis. And the intervention by the national government into the conduct of internal and foreign trade, including the use of measures of public ownership or control, empirically, as an alternate method for the reorganization and administration of industry, came to be accepted.

With the prolongation of the depression the conviction spread in Britain that the solution to the nation's economic problems required both a national conception and a planned effort. This was considered the rational approach to assure the efficient use of productive resources, to alleviate the more ruthless aspects of competition, and to distribute the national product more fairly. The impact of World War II hastened and expanded the transformation in British thinking along these lines. It came to be held generally that bold programs were needed to reorient the nation's economic structure and pattern of behavior in order to establish a society in which the government would assume responsibility for the welfare of the individual and for orderly national economic development.

Against this background nationalization in trade union policy expanded from an independent issue into a key element of a trade union philosophy oriented towards a wholesale reorganization of British society. This development gathered strength in the trade union movement along with the growing inclination to believe that socialistic policies were in accord with the grain of history. Confirmation of this belief was seen in the increasing usage of state authority to sup-

31

plement or counter economic forces in order to energize trade and industry. In terms of the problem of the labor market, nationalization to the trade union movement took on special significance as a device to eliminate competitive situations which resulted in degrading the condition of the workingman.

For organized labor as a whole, nationalization became deeply rooted in an all-embracing program of economic planning and fundamental social and industrial reform, focussed on the objective of full employment through collective action. More than any other labor objective, nationalization became symbolic of a synthesis of interest between trade unionism and political socialism, and the connection between political power and economic welfare. In terms of British socialism measures for nationalization were regarded as solutions designed to meet specific current economic problems while futhering the eventual establishment of a socialist society. In the stricter trade union sense, nationalization was offered as the only means through which there was any hope of reconstructing depressed industries in whose success workingmen had a vital stake in order to provide secure employment and a rising standard of living.

At the same time organized labor sought to convince non-socialists of its moderation, its practicality, its claim to being in the direct line of British historical evolution, and its ability to administer the government. Within this framework organized labor, balancing theoretical conceptions against the possibilities of their realization by constitutional political methods in the foreseeable future, expanded and detailed a program for the public ownership and control of great national industries and services regarded as the mainsprings of the economy.

During World War II, organized labor reached a new peak of political and industrial power. It became a decisive voice in industry and government. It was constrained by a sense of responsibility, but it remained conscious of its strength and was determined to prevent a repetition of the events of the inter-war years. Towards the conclusion of hostilities organized labor resumed its independent political course presented its proposals for post-war reconstruction, and won the support of many non-socialists unwilling to rely on conservative-oriented thinking to make a fresh start in peacetime economic and social affairs. Organized labor emerged for the first time with a clear electoral mandate and an overwhelming parliamentary working majority sufficient to enact its "socialistic" program of which certain nationalization measures were essential features.

COLLABORATION AND THE MODERATE METHOD

The National Strike, the depression, and World II reoriented British industrial relations. The revised attitudes of trade unions and employers were reflected in the dramatic decline in industrial warfare and in the elaboration of labor-management negotiations which increasingly became national in its considerations. In the process, the trade union movement sought new avenues to pursue its aspirations and to expand its influence on the course of economic and social policy. Thus it became committed on a widening scale to collaboration with employers and the government, not only in the traditional areas of industrial relations, but in the solution of other major problems facing the nation.

The TUC established definitively in its official policy and action that it had rejected revolutionary theories which taught that the workingman was locked in an irreconcilable struggle with his "capitalist" employer, or that organized labor was under a compulsion to use its industrial strength to undermine the functioning of the "capitalistic" economic system. On the other hand the trade unions were accepted, in a degree, as having an institutional right to a voice in the business of running industry and the country. Accordingly, having no desire to return to the days of bitter conflict, the trade union movement set out to obtain by negotiation and the benefit of circumstances ever-increasing influence in the administration of the state and industry. In doing so the trade union movement made it clear that whatever its political alliances and whatever the conception prevailing in its councils as to the most desirable form of society, it regarded the solution of current industrial problems in collaboration with employers and the government as the best method of representing the interests of the worker, improving his economic condition, and serving the nation as a whole.

While industrial militancy waned and negotiation reached a new prominence in labor-management relations, the leanings of the trade unions towards political solutions and the pressures which involved them in political affairs continued to grow. The political consciousness and the activity of the trade unions were stimulated by the broadening scope of government policies which affected them. Trade unions became more deeply involved in the internal controversies of the Labor Party as well as in partisan politics. Their interest and participation in international affairs grew with the rising tension in Europe and the Far East. With the consolidation and projection of its influence beyond its numbers, the trade union movement became decisive, and in major instances predominant, in shaping specific Labor Party policies in domestic and foreign affairs to which the third Labor government eventually became committed.

The approach to economic problems of British organized labor came to be guided more and more by a belief that the world had settled into a certain equilibrium in which heavy unemployment was inherent, and that Britain's particular ills could not be remedied without radical reconstruction. Having discarded revolutionary methods, organized labor settled on a policy of securing for the worker the best terms possible within the economic system as it existed. However, it also made itself the vanguard of a distinct trend to effect fundamental changes in society by giving the government decisive control over the forces of economic life.

Being committed to constitutional political methods, organized labor broadened its political acceptability to attract sympathetic support among those who, while having no special ties to labor, felt that the conservative approach to economic and social problems gave too much weight to the point of view of the businessman and failed to measure up to the human problems of the time. The progress of labor's effort to win national support was marked by its steady rise in electoral popularity after 1931 outdistancing by far the official membership of the Labor Party and trade union membership.

The Second World War enormously expanded the power of organized labor strategically and numerically. Also the popularity of labor's proposals for reform was fortified by a national determination not to repeat the experiences which followed World War I. The wartime crises, the scrapping of habitual modes of thought, and the national sweep of feeling for reconstruction expressed themselves in a spirit of planning for the reorientation of the British social and economic structure. Though the coalition government led by the Conservative Party had taken long strides in the direction of these goals, the post-war mood favored the prospects of the party associated in the popular mind with change and a fresh initiative. Many more people were prepared to contemplate radical changes with relative equanimity. Compared with a low vote of 6,363,000 and 46 seats in the House of Commons in 1931, the labor vote rose to 8,325,000 and 154 seats in 1935, and almost 12,000,000 votes and 392 seats in 1945.

PRAGMATIC SOCIALISM AND NATIONALIZATION

With all the dominant trends of political and economic thinking moving in the direction of centralization and the increasing participation of government in economic life, the British environment became more favorable and responsive to the idea of nationalization. Themes which stressed the advantages of various types of planning to achieve national economic efficiency and to solve the problem of mass unemployment became popular. The development of new tools of economic analysis and of intellectual conceptions, such as those of Keynes, which held that even a private enterprise state could decisively affect the level of employment and distribution of income, supplied powerful arguments for the idea that nations were not helpless against the workings of economic laws. This strengthened the tendency to regard the state less as a necessary evil and more as a constructive social and economic force. It also served to modify traditional principles of individual rights with respect to property and economic action.

Within the rather indistinct meaning of non-doctrinaire British socialism, organized labor also attracted many new supporters, though with their own interpretations. To many who accepted the designation socialist or were acknowledged sympathizers socialism meant the management of public policy with a superior consciousness of problems in their total effect on British society. They regarded certain aspects of a system based on the private ownership of the means of production as defying reform, and the solution offered by Conservatives and Liberals as futile. They regarded social and economic planning as the next stage in the development of human society. This appealed to them as a practical means of relieving the economy of the harshness of alternate booms and slumps and of abolishing involuntary unemployment.

These socialistic elements were disposed to consider their immediate aims in terms of protecting the worker and consumer against the unregulated impact of the open market, the abolition of heritages of privilege and human exploitation, the advancement of enlightened social welfare, labor, and foreign policies; and the nationalization of a large section of industry to achieve desired industrial efficiency and to effect public control over the economy. But they had no strong ideological views and were prepared to consider each question, including the question of public or private ownership, on its merits. In sum, they were critical of conservatism and orthodoxy but unwilling to commit themselves unequivocally to distant horizons. However,

within the area of reasoned experiment they were prepared to support
a particular program of social and economic reform. For this purpose the Labor Party seemed to them to be less inhibited and more
realistic than the Conservatives or Liberals.

Thus labor's nationalization policies showed the combined effects
of long-range social idealism, the resolution of internal differences
of conception among diverse elements in the labor movement, and the
compromises necessary to establish common ground with non-socialists and to explain to them in understandable terms in what way nationalization was a relevant and effective solution to certain national
problems.

Organized labor ranged itself more decisively than ever before
against the older political parties and orthodox economic thinking.
But it also curbed doctrinaire extremism in its ranks and took pains
in particular to dissociate its own British radical heritage from the
theory and practice of Communism. It compromised the diverse considerations of the members of the collectivist "labor alliance" in ac-
commodating its policies to the interests of the non-state collectivism
of the cooperatives, the functions of independent trade unionism, and
the aspirations of the state socialists. It did this within a framework of attempting to satisfy the realities of party political action, and
to establish a basis of continuity with existing experience.

Governed by these conditions of compromise and collaboration,
organized labor limited its demands for nationalization to those industries and services which the country seemed most ready to consider. It dealt with each case on its merits. It preferred to make
partial gains rather than risk making none at all.

In its formulations of nationalization, organized labor justified the
continued existence in a planned economy of private enterprise together with the public ownership and control of certain goods and
services. It advocated principles and methods of nationalization based
on precedents that had won general agreement in the political and
economic community as a whole—such as fair compensation, the non-
political autonomous administration of public enterprises, and the
supremacy of community over sectional interests. While advocating
nationalization on more "socialistic" lines, labor accepted and supported complete or partial ownership and control of industry
on terms satisfactory to non-socialists—as in radio broadcasting, electricity, transport, overseas airways, and coal. In other instances,
where conditions made it more practicable to obtain labor objectives
by other means, the idea of nationalization was set aside, as in the cases

of the distributive trades and cotton textiles. And during World War II British labor held in abeyance its long-standing demands for nationalization in the interests of the unity of the Coalition government.

NATIONALIZATION AND THE PUBLIC CORPORATION

As distinct from the controversies over the various proposals for public ownership after 1926, there were certain principles relative to the establishment of state enterprise which British socialists and non-socialists alike came to accept. Particularly significant was the concept of the public concern or the public corporation which came to be generally regarded as the most desirable administrative structure for a nationalized business.

The modern public corporation won approval in preference to the older type of public body run on the lines of a government department, such as the Post Office. The public corporation was considered the most suitable instrument for combining national ownership, expert management and the flexibility and initiative of private business. The precepts for the creation, organization and operation of government enterprises as worked out with reference to the public corporation broadly were as follows:

The public corporation was made subject to the rule of law. Where created by the government its property was to be purchased without penalty to the proprietors at a fair price. This would be decided by arbitration where the owners and government failed to agree. The management of the nationalized enterprise, while responsible to the minister answerable in Parliament on policy matters pertaining to the industry as a whole, was to be autonomous and kept free of direct parliamentary interference and partisan politics in its day-to-day operations. Salaries of the management and subordinate personnel were to be determined according to criteria relating to the enterprise rather than in relation to government salary schedules. The management and staff were to be selected solely on grounds of professional merit without regard to politics or ideological convictions. While the views of economic interests especially affected by the operation of the industry were to be given careful consideration, there was to be no statutory sectional representation.

Each member of the management was to be responsible for doing his duty only in terms of the community as a whole and was expected to divest himself of other obligations that could possibly result in a conflict of interest. Each public concern was to be autonomous in its internal functioning, including its financial and staffing policies. This meant its financial structure and labor-management relationships, for example, were to be determined by the circumstances of each enterprise rather than according to a prescribed formula.   Though profits were not to be its objective, and profits in any case were to be non-divisible, the concern was expected to be conducted in a business-like manner to achieve the highest standards of productive efficiency. With allowances for special conditions the public concern was expected to be self-supporting, averaging profitable and unprofitable years.

Under the various governments between 1926 and 1939 there were significant extensions of public ownership.   Though there was no single form, method, or motivation with respect to public ownership, these measures set precedents and established principles which were also embodied in the nationalization plans drawn up by British labor.

Central Electricity Board. Following the passage of the Electricity Supply Act of 1926 the Central Electricity Board (CEB) was established to bring about a centralized, standard electricity supply.   Earlier attempts at the end of World War I to establish a national grid to match the growth of industry had failed.   The measure grew out of the recommendations of the Weir Committee established under the Conservative Baldwin government to look into the problem.[1]

The direct control of the CEB was limited to the wholesale generation and transmission of electricity to retail distributors, more than half of which were local authorities, and the remainder were private companies.   Trading operations were started in 1930.   In this combination of public and private ownership, while the board was given authority to own transmission lines, which for the most part had to be constructed new, generating stations were to remain, at least formally, in the hands of private undertakers.   However, the CEB also was given certain powers to acquire or close down generating stations, fix grid tariffs, and other related authority to effect the standardization and uniformity of electricity supply nationally.

For purposes of parliamentary responsibility the CEB fell under the supervision of the Minister of Transport who appointed the members.   It was also subject to the general supervision of the Electricity Commission, the industry's regulatory body set up under the Electricity Act (1919).   Otherwise, the CEB operated as an autonomous authority with control over its own personnel and financial matters. Subject to certain supervision, it could engage in short term commercial borrowing and issue Central Electricity stock which the Treasury could guarantee.[2]

The managing board was composed of a chairman and seven members appointed for terms of five to ten years after consultation with representative bodies in the fields of local government, electricity, commerce, industry, transport, agriculture, and labor. But members had to detach themselves from possible sources of conflict of interest. This was as far as the government would concede to pressure for the specific representation of interests. The first chairman of the CEB was Sir Andrew Rae Duncan, a prominent figure in the business community and in the public service. His salary of £7,000 per annum far exceeded that of the Minister of Transport, for instance—a comparison that became typical with respect to other public concerns.

The CEB, a combination of public and private enterprise instituted by a Conservative government despite Conservative criticism of the scheme as a "socialistic" measure, came to be accepted as a success, and was incorporated into the completely nationalized electricity scheme in 1947.

British Broadcasting Corporation. The Conservative Baldwin government also converted radio broadcasting from private to public ownership. As of January 1, 1927 the British Broadcasting Corporation (BBC), established under a royal charter, took over what amounted to the broadcasting industry, i.e., the British Broadcasting Company. This was the ultimate result of the report of the Crawford Committee.[3]

The idea of a government-owned radio service had the non-partisan support of various public and private interests, including members of the radio manufacturing industry. Whereas the justification for public ownership in electricity, for example, had been found in more narrowly economic criteria, the control of radio raised problems of public policy in an embryonic industry which in the British view outweighed commercial considerations or questions of operating efficiency. In addition to concern over the excesses of commercial broadcasting which had acquired a bad reputation, the role played by radio during the National Strike had created a firm belief in British public opinion that the medium was of too great moment to be left in private hands. These feelings sustained the continuation of non-partisan support for state-owned radio broadcasting and the subsequent renewals of the BBC charter.

The government bought out the old company's subscribed share capital of £71,536 at par, and transferred the holdings to a wholly government-owned corporation. Control of operations was given to an independent public Board of Governors appointed by the Crown on the recommendation of the Prime Minister and the Postmaster General without regard to sectional interests. The BBC which was given in fact, if not in law, an exclusive monopoly of domestic and foreign radio broadcasting for Great Britain and Northern Ireland, was to be developed as a public service medium of information, education, and entertainment, free from political interference.

The radio service was not to be government-operated or administered directly. But the government retained wide contingent powers under the charter. It did this through a supplementary license issued by the Postmaster General who consequently assumed ultimate parliamentary responsibility. Nevertheless, the BBC received a large degree of autonomy in its finances and operated outside the civil service, establishing its own personnel policies. With occasional exceptions, the BBC was made dependent upon revenue for its expenditures, including those for capital investment. The income of the BBC was to be derived from fees paid to the Post Office by the owners of radio sets and by supplementary revenue derived from auxiliary activities, e.g., sales of its publications, applicable to the promotion of the objects of its charter.

Sir John Reith, who had been managing director of the old company, was appointed Director General of the BBC, serving until 1938. In 1936 the BBC charter, and supplementary license and agreement were renewed for another ten years.

London Passenger Transport Board. The unification of the London passenger transportation system was the product of a whole generation of thought and consideration. It was a first effort at public ownership by a Labor government, having been initiated by the minority MacDonald Labor government of 1931. This government, which was dependent on Liberal support, repudiated the scheme of the predecessor Conservative government for unification under predominantly private ownership. Nevertheless, the bill prepared by the Labor Minister of Transport, Herbert Morrison, to establish a transport monopoly under a public corporation, actually was a compromise Labor, Liberal, and Conservative measure. It was enacted in 1933 only after the continuous exertions of successive ministers from each of the three main political parties—Labor, Liberal, and Conservative, in that order.

The complex negotiations and political dueling that surrounded the passage of the London Passenger Transport bill served to reinforce the basic principle of the businesslike non-political management of a public enterprise. Unlike the case of other public corporations, the governing board was made largely independent of the Minister of Transport in order to attenuate possible political influence over appointments. Compensation for the private and local government transport systems that were taken over was fixed by agreement or by a special three member arbitration tribunal.

The seven man London Passenger Transport Board (LPTB), created to manage the business, for purposes of parliamentary responsibility came under the jurisdiction of the Minister of Transport. However, unlike the other public corporations the LPTB was established in the form of a public trusteeship as the Port of London Authority had been in 1908. In a sense this involved a departure from the principle of non-sectional representation since the members of the LPTB were appointed by six *ad hoc* appointing trustees drawn from prominent established community and economic interests.

As with other public corporations, the pattern of autonomy in financial and personnel affairs was maintained. However, statutory provision was made to carry over, with extensions, the consultative and collective bargaining machinery of the various London transport enterprises. The Transport and General Workers' Union (TGWU) did not win its demand that the authorizing legislation provide for the representation on the board of the unions in the industry. This existed *de facto* if not *de jure* on the Port of London Authority. Nevertheless, Mr. John Cliff, the TGWU assistant general secretary was appointed as a member with special part-time duties in connection with personnel matters. In turn he agreed to cease all his activities as a union officer for the duration of his membership on the board. Other members of the board similarly were required to withdraw from outside activities which could result in a conflict of interest.

The first chairman and vice-chairman of the LPTB were Lord Ashfield at £12,500 per annum and Mr. Frank Pick at £10,000 per annum. They had developed and had been chairman and managing director respectively of the privately-owned London underground (i.e., subways).

The LPTB took over the underground, buses, and trolleys lines July 1, 1933, with the purpose of establishing a single unified transport system that would be cheap, efficient, and financially sound, and would provide for an expansion of a non-competitive service to meet the growing needs of the city and suburbs of London. The LPTB was superseded in 1948 by the London Transport Executive under the integrated national transport system established by the Transport (Nationalization) Act of 1947.

The British Overseas Airways Corporation. The British Overseas Airways Corporation (BOAC) was the product of a change in traditional civil aviation policy—from one of developing British aviation by subvention under private ownership to that of the subsidy of a "chosen instrument" under public ownership. After two decades during which the government through legislation sought to encourage civil aviation development while retaining the principle of private ownership, the National government headed by Prime Minister Neville Chamberlain, a Conservative, legislated the BOAC into existence in August 1939 as a public corporation. This followed the report of a special commission which had recommended reorganization under private ownership. However the report also had sharply criticized the managements of the subsidized airlines—Imperial Airways and British Airways—and especially the debilitating competition between the companies on certain overseas routes.[4]

The statutory function of the BOAC was to secure in the national interest the fullest development of efficient overseas air transport services to be operated at reasonable charges. While BOAC embodied the characteristics of other public corporations, it was recognized that subsidies would be needed for some years to come. Consequently, unlike the others, no requirement was placed on it to pay its way out of revenue over a period of years. However, while it was given more independence in financial policies than the usual government department it was allowed less freedom in this respect than other public corporations. Also, statutory provision was made for the corporation to carry over the employees of the two predecessor corporations, engage in collective bargaining, and maintain the personnel standards of the "good employer."

After negotiation, the BOAC bought out Imperial Airways and British Airways for a combination of cash and a new series of Airways' stock. BOAC was given a monopoly of overseas air routes, and could engage in commercial activities relevant to its franchise. The board of BOAC was to consist of a chairman, vice-chairman, and from nine to fifteen members appointed at the discretion of the Secretary of State for Air. Sir John Reith who had acquired a commanding reputation for his stewardship of the BBC was appointed the first chairman of the BOAC. However, before the corporation could begin to operate as scheduled in April, 1940, war broke out, and the corporation was placed under the operational control of the Air Ministry.

Under the Civil Aviation Act of 1946 BOAC was incorporated into the nationalized system of domestic and overseas air services.

Coal and the Nationalization of Royalties. The controversies which continued over the reorganization of the coal industry led successive governments to enact a series of measures which it was hoped would promote unification, alleviate the fierce competition in the industry, and reduce costs. This policy was based on fairly general agreement that in most years the industry was working below its capacity, yielding less than a fair return to labor and to the capital invested in it, and that the reorganization of the industry was essential to national prosperity. In dealing with these problems the government's role remained essentially one of exerting pressure and offering incentives to private owners to effect amalgamation, in preference to one of assuming direct control and ownership of the industry. Though this approach had little effect on the reorganization of the industry or the improvement of its efficiency, it led eventually to the disposition of one major issue—namely, the nationalization of coal royalties. This measure, of Liberal and Labor parentage, was legislated in 1938 by the Conservative-oriented National government headed by Prime Minister Neville Chamberlain.

In August 1926, during the mining strike, the Baldwin government passed the previously mentioned Mining Industry Act. The act sought to encourage the amalgamation of existing firms and established machinery to overcome the objections of minority interests unwilling to be absorbed by such schemes. The initiative under the scheme was expected to come from mine owners. While some amalgamations were concluded, they were of practically no effect on the industry as a whole.

Four years later the minority MacDonald Labor government, in the spirit of "rationalization" and the trend away from competition in British industry, passed the Coal Mines Act. The measure, drafted after consultation with the coal owners and the Miners' Federation sought to break the traditional pattern of ruthless competition in the industry. It sought in this way to end the historical policy of the coal fields— that of price cutting to halt slumping sales and profits by a simple direct attack on labor costs, i.e. by reducing wage rates. The new policy was based on a belief that in view of the international depression in the industry there was an inelastic demand for coal which for the time being made it idle to hope for an expansion of coal sales even at very low prices. The act, which made concessions to Liberal supporters and Conservative opponents, provided for centralized ma-

chinery, to be established by the colliery owners, to fix minimum prices
and to regulate and allocate the production and sale of coal. Penalties
could be imposed on mines for non-compliance with quota limitations.

Also, a five member Coal Mines Reorganization Commission
(CMRC) was established with compulsory powers to bring about the
amalgamation of collieries into more economic units. But the legal
entanglements arising from the interpretation of the powers of the
CMRC eventually stymied any effective operation of this part of the
act and any significant reorganization of the industry which might
have flowed from it. The statutory shift for underground miners,
extended to eight hours after the National Strike, was reduced to
seven and one half. But an attempt to set up under the act a Coal
Mines National Industrial Board to stabilize labor-management relations and place the wage structure on a national basis, suffered a fate
analogous to the amalgamation sections of the act, and became a dead
letter.

The act, after a slow start, was successful eventually in cartelizing
the industry, but it had little effect in bringing about the desired
amalgamation and reorganization, or the alleviation of labor-management antagonisms. Cartelization in these circumstances became a
device to protect the weak and inefficient producer.[5]

Eventually, the Chamberlain government passed the Coal Mines
Act (1938) nationalizing royalties, i.e., payments to owners of coal-
bearing lands by colliery companies for the privilege of operating
mines. A special arbitration board fixed the amount of remuneration
to be paid to the owners of royalties at £66,450,000, and this sum
was written into the law as the amount to be apportioned among royalty owners. The principle of valuation was that existing owners
should not be penalized by the loss of reasonably expected future
income. Compensation for individual properties was to be determined
by valuation boards set up for the purpose.

The act also transferred the functions of the former CMRC to a new
Coal Commission which also took possession of the royalty rights as
a public corporation. On the new five-member commission, appointed
by the President of the Board of Trade, no provision was made for
sectional representation except that two members were required to be
persons with practical experience in the coal mining industry, one of
them in the capacity of a wage earner.

The commission, which became the recipient of royalties from less-
ees, was to administer its holdings in such a way as its members considered best for promoting the efficiency and better organization of the

coal industry. It could make recommendations and be empowered by the Board of Trade to carry out schemes of amalgamation and re-organization. It could not engage in coal mining itself except for its exclusive right to search and bore for coal. The commission was to be self-contained financially, with its own accounts in a separate "coal fund." It could set the rents for leases, borrow money under regulations laid down by the Board of Trade and the Treasury, and issue and redeem Coal Commission stock on which principal and interest could be guaranteed by the Treasury.

Taken over the entire period,[e] apart from the trends of costs and prices, the layout of the coal industry changed little, notwithstanding the reorganization legislation of the inter-war years. Though the 1938 act brought British law into line with that of most other coal-possessing countries, its bearing on the efficiency of the industry was only brief and indirect. Under the act the established mining operations which conformed to the rights and boundaries of private estates on the surface remained almost unaltered since, broadly speaking, leases in force at the time of transfer were unchanged except for the change of lessor. In any case, under the statute the commission's work on amalgamation had not been scheduled to begin until January 1, 1940, and the transfer of royalty rights was not completed until 1942—by which time the Churchill Coalition government as a war measure had taken over complete control of the mines.

The state of the industry as Britain entered World War II has been summed up in an official government history as follows: "The coal industry in 1939 was not unprofitable, but unlike that of 1914, it was depressed and contracting. . . . It was faced by two developing problems. Firstly, after many years of heavy unemployment and low wages the industry was nearing the time when it would have to take special measures to attract the labor which it needed, if it were to counteract the effects of the retirement of older men and the increasing disinclination of the young to enter it. Secondly, the efficiency of coal mining labor was coming to be below the best standards of current mining practice and to raise it would require heavy capital investment and a thorough overhaul of organization and technique. The money wanted for this purpose could only come to a limited extent from the colliery companies, while the outside investor was chary of touching enterprises which had a name for unprofitability and embittered industrial relations. . . .

"It was becoming clear that the mines could never afford a decent standard of life . . . partly because of the changes in the economic conditions of coal mining . . . and partly because . . . of altered notions of a decent living among working people as a whole.

"A persistent and confused conflict was going on between what the mine management and the mine worker and the vague mass of public opinion deemed right and proper and what actually existed. From this conflict the three parties concerned often found relief by throwing the whole blame upon one another.

"More perhaps than most industries, the coal industry represented in September, 1939, the testing ground for the weakness of the British economy and society."[7]

WORKING OUT LABOR'S NATIONALIZATION POLICIES

Between the National Strike and the outbreak of World War II the TUC and Labor Party systematically detailed and expanded a trade union-socialist program. This program drew its main force from the indignation caused by heavy unemployment and a strong faith in what could be accomplished by the national government through the public ownership and control of key industries and services. While the specific courses of action decided upon were moderate, the policies arrived at reflected a fundamental radicalization of thought and expression in British organized labor. The form and major principles of nationalization were worked out by the political and industrial wings of the labor movement between 1931 and 1936. They were incorporated into successive individual plans for nationalization and eventually into the program for post-war reconstruction drafted as World War II drew to a close.

After Nineteen Twenty-Six. In the years immediately following the National Strike, the trade union movement gave low priority to nationalization in comparison with the whole problem of taking inventory of its functions and status, and the reorientation of its thinking on basic industrial policy. In particular, the TUC was preoccupied with schisms and disruptions, its weakened moral, legal, and economic position, and the obligations of supporting a minority Labor government for the second time. For the most part nationalization received comparatively little attention and took a back seat to other issues such as the Mond-Turner conferences on labor-management collaboration, problems of deflation, conflicts with communists in the domestic and international labor sphere, and organizational problems stemming from the decline of union membership and the residue of recriminations remaining from the National Strike.

Initiating the "Modernization" of Policy. It was not until the 1931 trades union congress that a full-blooded debate opened on ideas of planning and public ownership. Dominated by the excitement of the sudden fall of the Labor government a month earlier, and the impact of the deepening world financial crisis, the TUC embarked on a long-range appraisal and bolder formulation of policies, "modernized" to suit contemporary political and economic conditions. The congress laid the ground-work or initiated debates on specific aspects of nationalization on the widest scale since World War I. Most significant was the passage of a resolution which became the authorization in subsequent years for the various nationalization plans which the TUC drew up in conjunction with the Labor Party. Entitled "Planning" the resolution, moved by Arthur Pugh (general secretary of the Iron and Steel Trades Confederation) and Ernest Bevin (general secretary of the Transport and General Workers Union), declared:

"This Congress, being in accord with the traditional policy of the Trade Union Movement, welcomes the present tendency towards a planned and regulated economy in our national life.

"Having regard to the seriousness of the economic situation, Congress expresses the view that only by a comprehensive planning of our economic development, and regulated trading relations, can the needs of the present day be met.

"Congress therefore instructs the General Council boldly to advance this policy both nationally and internationally, keeping in mind that in order to maintain and improve the standard of living, the people as consumers must be protected by public control and regulation from exploitation."[8]

In moving the resolution on behalf of the General Council, Arthur Pugh told the congress: "The purpose of the resolution is to emphasize the importance of our Trade Union Movement, through its Annual Congress, formulating a practical policy in relation to the national economic life, and in regard to international trading and commercial relations between this and other countries of the world. . . . While we have obtained the machinery of a political democracy, we have on the other hand what is virutally an economic autocracy."[9]

At this congress the differences within the labor movement over the aforementioned London Transport bill, framed by Herbert Morrison when he was Minister of Transport in the fallen Labor government, led to the first open controversy within the TUC over the

meaning and application of "workers' control." The Transport and
General Workers Union had insisted that trade unions should
have direct representation on the management of nationalized industries, a demand that Morrison previously had rejected when Minister
of Transport. The congress carried the TGWU resolution over opposition which included the General Council and the National Union
of Railwaymen, which had members on the London underground
also. The opposition warned that special representation of trade
unions would open the way to demands for similar representation by
"capitalist" interests which would consequently outnumber the labor
representation on nationalized boards. This argument was raised
in addition to other objections that by providing such representation
boards would become bodies of conflicting interests rather than co-
hesive managements. Actually, however, the congress left the issue
in abeyance. The congress agreed that the practical application of
the principle should be left to the General Council for further examination and that the General Council should report the following
year after examining the implications of the principle in conjunction
with the Labor Party.[10]

The same congress in comprehensive resolutions also reaffirmed
its demand for nationalization of the coal mines; and it authorized
the General Council to draft plans for the reorganization of the nation's transport and iron and steel industries under public ownership.
But as to the nationalization of industrial insurance, there was no
agreement. The spokesman for the General Council explained why
the TUC and Labor Party had not arrived at an agreed formula,
since "It is a much bigger question than appeared. . . . We have so
many vested interests in the trade unions. . . . I admit we were not
agreed amongst ourselves and particularly between members of the
Trades Union Congress and Labor Party."[11]

The Principles of 1932. With organized labor at the lowest ebb
of its economic and political fortunes and unemployment at its worst,
the TUC for the first time in its history undertook a comprehensive
consideration of the question of the relationships of trade unionism
to the public control of industry. A report, entitled "The Public
Control and Regulation of Industry and Trade,"[12] was prepared in
close consultation with the Labor Party and became the basic trade
union document on nationalization. Its purpose was to "redefine the
aims of the movement in connection with socialization of industry
in the light of modern conditions."[13] In a broad sense, this report
was complementary in the domestic sphere to a "Report on Fiscal

Policy,"[14] which dealt in non-doctrinaire socialist fashion with Britain's economic problems with particular attention to the regulation of Britain's foreign trade as an alternative to either free trade or protectionism.

The report on "The Public Control and Regulation of Industry and Trade" was presented to the 1932 congress in the hope of its being adopted in time for the Labor Party conference scheduled for the following month. Despite the atmosphere of world economic crisis which encouraged thoughts that a major transformation in the economic and social order was in the making, the report was not drafted with the expectation that its ideas for socialization would soon materialize. Its purpose, the report stated, was to lay down general principles for the "transitional forms of public control and the immediate steps to be taken rather than the more ideal programme of complete socialization."[15]

In accordance with this "gradual" approach to nationalization the report divided industries and services into three categories: those immediately ripe for nationalization; those less important needing some regulation; and those of minor importance which could be left for the time being completely under private ownership.

The report admitted that the decision as to whether an industry fell into one or the other of these classifications was bound to be arbitrary, that the determination as to what businesses were "affected with a public interest" would be a difficult one, and that "the progress from private enterprise to public control depends really upon the state of public opinion."[16] Nevertheless, the report did suggest criteria for socialization or control: the importance of an industry or service to the life and safety of the community; the existence of monopoly or unification in an industry or service serving a wide demand; or the importance of an industry as a source of demand for new investment. To secure the various gradations of public control the report recommended either complete nationalization and operation by the government, the financial and directive participation by the government in private enterprise, or the regulation of selected industries through legislation.

In adopting this report the TUC set aside the concept of the government department and the fiscal and staff controls associated with it in favor of the independent public corporation. It emphasized that public enterprises should be self supporting. It also rejected confiscation in favor of fair compensation, the determination of which would depend on the general circumstances prevailing at the time of socialization. To criticism that nationalization by purchase with government-backed securities would only serve to guarantee rather than socialize the income of former owners the report noted, "This disadvantage may be counteracted by taxation."[17]

To give workers a voice in industrial policy, the TUC proposed labor-management collaboration through a comprehensive system of joint consultation and the maintenance of free collective bargaining in nationalized industries. Opposing the idea of "workers' control" in the syndicalist or guild socialist sense of the term, or as trade union representation in the management, the report took the position that "while members may be drawn from different classes of the community (e.g. labor, business, administration), particular interests should not nominate members but should rather be represented on Advisory or Consultative Boards."[18] In the face of strong opposition led by the TGWU this statement of "workers' control" was set aside while the remainder of the report was adopted.

This same congress urged the immediate passage of the London Passenger Transport bill,[19] and "the planning of large scale developments . . . and other public works which will provide long-term employment and improved purchasing power for persons now employed, the public control of banking and monopolistic industries, and the taxation of land values."[20]

Indicating the unity of its views with organized labor in other countries which shared its socialistic analysis of the impasse in which economic activity throughout the world seemed to be gripped, the TUC endorsed a resolution on the world unemployment crisis passed at the Sixth Ordinary Congress of the International Federation of Trade Unions (IFTU). The resolution declared in part: "A beginning must also be made with the transformation of the economic system. The experience of the last few years shows very plainly that the tendency of the world is to form large economic units. Parallel with the complete transformation of the world, there must therefore be an extension of public enterprise in all the important spheres of economic life."[21]

A month later at the Labor Party conference the TGWU again pressed its demand for trade union representation on the managements of nationalized enterprises. However, compared with its resolution at the trades union congress which had preceded, the TGWU proposal at the Labor Party conference was modified somewhat to read that certain members of the managing authority "shall be appointed by the Minister only after consultation with the Trades Unions having members in the industry."[22]

The debate on this issue at the conference was marked by a sharp personal clash of views between Morrison and Bevin over trade union representation with respect to the then proposed LPTB. Morrison in opposing the TGWU demand for trade union representation on the LPTB argued: "The London County Council . . . agrees with the Transport Workers' Union. . . . They know that once they concede to Labor the right of representation they can get all their pals on the Board and swamp it with non-labor elements . . . in all probability Tory."[23]

Bevin by way of response complained that there had been inadequate consultation with the trade unions concerned with the London Passenger Transport bill, and charged that even the former Labor government had kept them at a distance while framing the bill. "In our view," said Bevin, "Mr. Morrison was determined to force his point of view through, and I hope that I have some views on the construction and management of industry from experience I obtained equally with him."[24]

However, the National Executive Committee prevailed upon the TGWU to withdraw its demand and leave open the whole question of "workers' control" for further consideration in conjunction with the General Council.[25] Thus the effect of the developments of 1932 was to leave the TUC and Labor Party undecided on the issue of "workers' control" while establishing as official labor policy the other principles embodied in the General Council's report and the special companion reports of the Labor Party.

The "Workers' Control" Debate. "Workers' control" remained the most controversial aspect of nationalization within the ranks of labor.

A memorandum drafted in 1933 jointly by the General Council and Labor Party National Executive Committee in order to secure uniformity of policy rejected the idea that trade unions should be given representation by statute on the boards of management of nationalized industry. Instead it restricted itself to claiming the right for the trade unions to nominate persons for the minister to consider for appointment. The memorandum on the "Public Control and Regulation of Industry"[26] stated that it was expected "that such boards would normally include persons from the Trade Union Movement who by their ability and knowledge were especially suitable for these posts," and that for this purpose "there should be consultation between the responsible Minister and the Trade Unions concerned."[27]

The memorandum warned against trade union participation in management, emphasizing the essentially professional nature of management in modern industry and the dangers which dual and possibly conflicting obligations held for the independence and internal harmony of trade unions. The definition of "workers' control" in the memorandum, while being accepted by the trades union congress that year, was rejected by the Labor Party conference by a narrow margin. The party conference insisted on "direct representation through trade unions, secured by statute, on the board of direction and control and other administrative bodies in the industry and service."[28]

These official differences were reconciled by 1935 when both bodies ratified a definition of "workers' control" which without further elaboration claimed that "the right of workers' organizations to be represented on the Governing Boards of socialized industries and services should . . . be secured by statute."[29] Thus while the issue of statutory obligation had been resolved for the time being, the meaning of "workers' control" remained the subject of interpretations and adaptations which ranged from syndicalist conceptions of industry run by the workers through their trade unions or elected boards, to proposals that were limited to trade union particicipation in labor-management consultative machinery.

In succeeding years while "workers' control" as a principle continued to be advocated as official policy by British labor leaders no decision was made by the TUC until 1944 as to how it was proposed to implement it. On the whole, however, the dominant trend was away from sectional representation on the boards of nationalized industry. None of the nationalization plans proposed by the TUC and Labor Party in the 1930's provided for trade union representation in the management. Rather, the various schemes emphasized the independence of management by trade unions as the best safeguard of workers' interests, the appointment of board members based on merit, and the sovereign power of the community interest exercised through Parliament over nationalized industry.

By 1944, in the "Interim Report on Post-War Reconstruction" the interpretation given to the "workers' control" principle was one that specified the statutory obligation as being the right of the TUC to nominate trade unionists for consideration by the government for appointments to boards.[30] In 1945 the TUC endorsed the following summation as the settled policy of organized labor with respect to "workers' control": "Briefly, these views are as follows: (a) that the two Movements desire public control of industry rather than workers' control as such; (b) that public control of industry is a means towards efficiency and, therefore, the Governing Boards of publicly-owned industries should be appointed on the basis of competence and ability to run the industry efficiently in the public interest; and (c) that in the making of statutory provisions for the appointment to Governing Boards of persons with experience and knowledge of workpeople's interests care should be taken to avoid the creation of dual responsibility."[31]

In 1946, in connection with legislation for coal nationalization, the statutory obligation was dropped in favor of an assurance by the Labor government that the minister and trade unions concerned would consult on pertinent appointments.[32]

Other Plans and Principles. In the years that followed, until the outbreak of World War II, British organized labor drafted several plans for public ownership and control and made periodic decisions of principle with respect to the basic report of 1932. The concepts of that report were incorporated into schemes for the socialization of iron and steel (1934),[33] cotton textiles (1935),[34] and coal (1936).[35] The declared purposes of these plans were to reorganize and stabilize these industries to eliminate the heavy chronic underemployment of labor and capital resources and bolster their competitive position in world markets. The plans also proposed to eliminate competitive practices within the industry that were a constant threat to wage and living standards.

In 1936 the TUC presented a plan to carry to completion the nationalization of electricity supply[36] in order to achieve integration and standardization on a national scale. The TUC also endorsed the Labor Party's program for the reorganization and development of water supply by the national government.[37] At various congresses and conferences steps were taken as well which eventually led to the labor policy for a comprehensive social insurance scheme.[37a]

However, occasional resolutions for engineering nationalization (1933) led to no specific plan. Discussions of nationalization of insurance that arose periodically were sidetracked. The TUC also rejected suggestions for the socialization of distribution or for the licensing of retail trading which the cooperatives felt might become devices to stifle their growth. Instead, the TUC urged the establishment of a distributive trades board under the Trade Boards Act to stabilize and alleviate depressed employment conditions in the industry,[39] and afterwards dropped this demand in favor of achieving these ends through direct collective bargaining.[40]

When the government nationalized royalties under the Coal Mines (Unification of Royalties) Act 1938, the Labor Party accepted rather than opposed the bill when its amendments for complete nationalization were defeated. Similarly, the TUC shelved indefinitely its cotton socialization scheme in 1937. The TUC turned the question back to the United Textile Factory Workers' Association[41] which was engaged in negotiations with the government and employers to stabilize and regulate the industry in order to keep competition from being carried on at the expense of the worker. These negotiations led to the Cotton Industry (Reorganization) Act (1939) which the outbreak of war made largely inapplicable.

In addition to concern with various nationalization plans, the TUC made key decisions of principle. The TUC and Labor Party rejected doctrinaire proposals for nationalization by near-confiscation rather than by fair compensation to the former owners. A memorandum, "Public Ownership and Compensation,"[42] endorsed by both the TUC and the Labor Party pointed to the dangers, impracticality, and injustices of confiscation. Emphasizing "gradualism" and the fundamental necessity of public sanction the policy statement declared: "When . . . the community decides in the public interest to resume possession of any part of the capital wealth of the country there is no question that it has the right to require from individuals surrender of some part of the privileges which the State has hitherto accorded to them. The choice of method is all important, however, in order that the transition to Socialism may be effected as smoothly, as efficiently, and as rapidly as possible. For this purpose, it is desirable (1) that there shall not be any greater break with the past than is necessary for the purpose, and (2) that as between individuals the State shall act in a way which appears to the ordinary man and woman reasonable and just."[43]

The TUC also repeatedly emphasized the democratic conception of its socialist orientation. Thus it regularly rejected periodic maneuvers to join in a "united front" with the communists against various domestic and international fascist activities. In this regard the TUC summed up its policy in a special resolution entitled the Failure of Capitalism and the Maintenance of Democracy: "We reaffirm our complete faith in the principles of Socialism and democracy. We believe that the world cannot be reconstructed by methods of violence and suppression, and the Congress therefore pledges itself to work whole-heartedly for the maintenance of free institutions, liberty of speech, of the Press, of public meeting, and the right of association. We set our face against any kind of dictatorship as being false to those devoted pioneers, whose sacrifices have brought us so far on the road to the democratic State to be reached by an improved and vigorous Parliamentary system."[44]

On the question of statutory negotiating machinery in nationalized industries, the TUC declared: "It is undesirable and impracticable to specify any one particular form of negotiating machinery for all such industries."[45] And British labor made clear its attitude on the matter of the political beliefs of the management of publicly-owned enterprises during the debate over the renewal of the BBC charter. Contrary to the traditional doctrinaire socialist approach which identified social, political, and economic interest, and therefore reasoned that the governors of nationalized enterprises must be socialist to give birth to a new order, the National Council of Labor speaking for the TUC, the Labor Party, and the Parliamentary Labor Party took the opposite view. In supporting its own complaint that the BBC was dominated by a Board of Governors oriented towards the Conservative Party and orthodox economic views, and in demanding the equal treatment of the views of organized labor, the council reaffirmed its support of the principle of the non-partisan, non-ideological administration of government undertakings, especially as applied to broadcasting.[46]

THE IMPACT OF WORLD WAR II

The experiences of World War II strengthened decisively the pressures for the public control or ownership of industry. The habits conditioned by war-time controls, the magnified influence of organized labor, and the sense of urgency which permeated the planning for the inevitable problems of post-war reconstruction contributed substantially to the reorientation of national thinking on immediate questions of social control. In a more fundamental sense, it can be said, that the controlling currents of British political opinion—including all the major political parties—had come to accept the idea that the government had a special responsibility for guiding the economy. Winston Churchill, Prime Minister, and by that time also leader of the Conservative Party, substantiated this view in 1943 during a broadcast to the nation on the problems of peace and reconstruction. While reaffirming his general opinion that a revival of "healthy and

vigorous private enterprise" at the earliest possible moment was vital
for Britain to achieve her post-war aims, he also announced that "A
number of measures are being and will be prepared which will enable
the Government to exercise a balancing influence upon developments
which can be turned on or off as circumstances require.   There is a
broadening field for state ownership and enterprise, especially in
relation to monopolies of all kinds."[47]

In particular, a considerable measure of national support developed
during the war for the public ownership of certain industries and
services, and this prepared the way for nationalization legislation to
become a prominent feature of Britain's post-war reconstruction
program.

In the cases of railways and mining the war proved to be the cata-
lyst in forestalling the return of control to their private owners and
brought about the final transformation of public opinion in favor of
nationalization—a quarter of a century after the issue had become
active during the First World War.   There was general agreement
at the end of the war that the British transport system, especially the
railways, needed large-scale capital expenditures for new equipment
and for the repair of other transport facilities, such as docks, on a
mass scale.   What was also needed was the rationalization of the
various transport services which were often competing in an economically wasteful manner.   Thus the future operation of road and
canal traffic, largely taken over by the government during the war,
in turn became tied to the fate of the railways and the whole question of an integrated transport system.   On this basis the Labor Party
eventually had its way despite the vigorous opposition of the Conservative and Liberal Parties to the labor scheme for the nationalization and integration of transport (and particularly road haulage)
which they doubted very much would make transport cheaper and
more efficient.

With respect to coal, the industry had been in a state of constant
crisis during the war, and this had led to a steady tightening of government control over its operations.   During the war the number of
producing mines had continued to fall, as did manpower and productivity.   Compared with 231,338,000 tons of saleable coal produced
in 1938, tonnage by 1943 fell to 194,500,000 and by 1945 to 174,658,000.[48]
As the end of the war approached there was no disagreement on the
post-war need for a complete economic and physical reorganization
of the coal industry.   This was summed up by the Reid Committee,
a group of seven eminent mining engineers appointed under the

Coalition government to survey the industry and make basic recommendations for its future efficiency. Without specifically recommending nationalization the committee had concluded "that it is not enough to recommend technical changes which we believe to be fully practicable, when it is evident to us, as mining engineers, that they cannot be satisfactorily carried through by the industry organized as it is today. . . . An Authority must be established which would have the duty of insuring that the industry is merged into units of such sizes as would provide the maximum advantage of planned production, of stimulating the preparation and execution of the broad plans of reorganization made by these units, and of conserving the coal resources of the country. The existence of such an Authority, endowed by Parliament with really effective powers for these purposes is, we are satisfied, a cardinal necessity."[49]

The colliery owners, towards the end of the war, had drawn up their own proposals for reorganization of the industry under private ownership.[50] But organized labor, and a decisive section of independent public opinion, had become convinced that the owners could never of their own volition bring about the drastic changes needed. Politically, although all parties agreed that reorganization was mandatory, the Labor and Liberal Parties favored nationalization, while the Conservative Party did not—and each party took its stand accordingly during the 1945 general election campaign.

Wartime exigencies contributed substantially to win public support for labor's long-standing contention that only by completing the process of national ownership and coordination could the electricity supply industry be "tidied up," reorganized, and expanded. Several years before the war, in May 1936, a detailed report by the McGowan Committee on Electricity Distribution, appointed by the Minister of Transport, had recommended the greater coordination of electricity supply and transmission. It had urged the compulsory creation of larger and more economic units, dismissed the alternatives of complete reorganization on a regional basis, and recommended a gradual absorption of the less efficient undertakings by the more efficient. It opposed complete ownership and national control by the government as proposed by the TUC. But the committee's report left the way open for this by declaring that "the schemes for reorganization should make provision for the possibility of ultimate public ownership of all undertakings."[51]

The government later drafted bills for the reorganization of electricity supply retaining the principle of private enterprise, although it made concessions to the trade unions which had protested its deference to private undertakings. But the outbreak of war in 1939 ended any further progress with the measure. In 1943, however, the public control of electricity supply advanced again when the North of Scotland Hydro-Electric Board was established to develop water power in the far north. By the end of the war the view that there was a need for large-scale capital investment to expand electricity plant and reorganize the nation's consumption of fuel and power more economically was unchallenged. What was more, the success of the Central Electricity Board had provided the precedent for the extension of the government role in this area.

As for gas, continuing the series of pre-war investigations, the Minister of Fuel and Power in 1944, appointed an independent and expert Committee of Inquiry headed by Geoffrey Heyworth, Chairman of the Board of Lever Bros. Ltd. In its report the following year the Gas Industry Committee declared that unification and rationalization of the gas industry was necessary for greater efficiency. It recommended nationalization as the best way to accomplish this.[52] This view was in accordance with the immediate policy of the Labor government and its general objective of establishing a coordinated national fuel and power supply at all levels under public ownership.

While the government-owned BOAC had continued during the war as the overseas civil air transport service, the majority of the seventeen licensed domestic airways which had been taken over by the Directorate of Civil Aviation had been closed down. Their routes had been reorganized on more essential lines. Early in 1945 the Coalition government announced the "Swinton Plan"[53] proposing the creation of three non-competing corporations with the government in partnership with private transportation interests, i.e. railways, shipping lines, and travel agencies. After the general election that year, the Labor government submitted a plan[54] proposing a similar general structure to encompass domestic and overseas airways but based on the complete public ownership of the three airways corporations. Exceptions were made for charter and taxi operations and club flying under private auspices.

There were still differences over private versus national interests on land tenure at the end of the war. But the issue of land nationalization, which for so many years had been the subject of keen political controversy, in the main had resolved itself into the general acceptance of the idea that the national government should plan the course of future land development. The Coalition government had established a Ministry of Town and Country Planning in 1943. The ministry carried forward studies of the problems of the purchase and public control of the use of the land, the means of preventing land speculation at the end of the war from hampering reconstruction, and particularly the planning of the physical rehabilitation of towns and the countryside.[55] The Coalition government started on its way the series of enactments completed in the post-war period which endowed the government with permanent powers to deal with the problems of land use.

Over the Bank of England there was little noticeable controversy since it was considered that nationalization would merely confirm the bank's *de facto* evolution into an instrument of financial administration of the central government. The idea of nationalizing overseas telecommunication services between Britain, the Dominions, and India was put forward by the 1944 Commonwealth Conference. A more definite scheme was recommended by another Commonwealth Conference the next year. As in the case of the Bank of England there was no opposition to what eventually amounted to a formal shift to public ownership of an already public-minded service.

The idea of a comprehensive, government-operated social insurance system was the subject of intense study and widespread national discussion during the war and became a sort of symbol of a new and better post-war world. As will be shown later, the final scheme, which included the extension and nationalization of all statutory social insurance, was the product of general agreement as represented in the Coalition government.

However, the idea of nationalization of the steel industry, which had been under a measure of public control since 1933, had to contend with determined opposition from the industry and independent public criticism. Moreover, there were doubts within organized labor itself as to what purpose would be served by nationalization in view of the changed circumstances since labor first proposed steel nationalization in 1943 as a means of lifting the steel industry out of a depressed state. The industry had become prosperous and was expanding, and the technical justification as to what would be accomplished by nationalization was a matter of intense controversy. The legislation by the time it was proposed by the Labor government in 1949 essentially consisted of a nominal transfer to the state of the industry as it existed—an act that served to minimize the complications of denationalizing the industry by the Conservative government after 1953.

By the end of the war, organized labor argued more strongly than ever that the national wartime crisis had vindicated its faith. It claimed that the nation had been compelled to apply socialistic principles in place of free enterprise and that a continued socialist approach was needed for the anticipated post-war crisis. The Conservative position was one of opposition to nationalization. The Liberal Party, while not going as far as the Labor Party, agreed that there should be nationalization of electric power, mining, railways and railway-controlled road transport undertakings, and state action to bring about land reform.

However, there was agreement among all parties that while the wartime apparatus of control could not be maintained, neither could all war-time controls be scrapped as soon as the emergency was over. Rather, controls would have to be re-examined and redesigned in the light of a possibly monumental economic crisis. Similarly, there was no quarrel with the premise that the postwar situation would call for large changes in the structure of British industry and trade, not merely in the transition from war to peace, but permanently. In this context, a week before the 1945 general election, in presenting its views as to what it believed the next Parliament should do, the London *Economist*, while critical of the doctrinaire factor in labor's demand for nationalization, urged the "planned reorganization of key industries, of which coal, steel and cotton should be the first on the list. The reorganization should follow strictly technical lines and questions of ownership should be settled on their merits. In coal, the element of public ownership and management would inevitably be large, in cotton small, with steel about midway between the other two. Transport and Power are two industries in which the benefits of a greater community of interest between what are now separate parts should be futher canvassed; until the results of these enquiries are clear, more changes of ownership or management of the separate parts would serve no useful purpose."[56]

The agreement on the need for planning on a national scale, which would endow the state with new and expanding industrial functions, made the atmosphere more favorable to organized labor's appeal to the electorate—that is, that a reconstruction program in postwar Britain must bring about a real social and economic change, end the "anarchy of production," extend democracy into economic affairs through the public control of industry, and head off another postwar depression.

PLANNING FOR POST-WAR RECONSTRUCTION

During World War II, the trade union movement collaborated with the government over a range of activity and with a measure of influence that dwarfed its previous experience a quarter of a century before. At the same time, the TUC at its wartime congresses continued the development of its policies at an accelerated pace along socialistic lines. While the TUC concentrated its energies on the more immediate problems of the war effort, almost from the beginning of hostilities the concern with postwar reconstruction also made itself apparent in British labor thinking especially with reference to labor's determination to prevent repetition of the post-World War I boom and collapse and a reversion of Britain to the economic condition of the inter-war years.

The wartime congresses were dominated by the pervasive influence of the immediate national emergency. Thus, the 1939 congress whose scheduled opening fell on the day after Britain declared war on Germany, was abbreviated to two days. All resolutions on the agenda were remitted to the General Council. In any event, the emergency atmosphere and crystallization of patriotic feeling precluded the discussion or public exhibition of differences on major questions.

The following year with the Battle of Britain underway following the collapse of France, the entire business of the congress was again concerned with mobilizing the fullest support for the war by organized labor—which by now through the Labor Party had become a participant in the Coalition government. Nevertheless, the congress did go on record as opposed to the return of railways to private control after the war and urged nationalization instead[57] The congress also gave expression to one of the guiding thoughts in its approach to post-war reconstruction. It called on the General Council "to prepare plans in advance to meet a possible slump . . . [and] that when these plans are prepared they be submitted to the country."[58]

In 1941, the TUC was virtually completely preoccupied with the swift turn of events following the German invasion of Russia. Nevertheless it ventured somewhat farther into the consideration of the problems of post-war reconstruction. In connection with the 1940 resolution the General Council reported that it had participated in preliminary discussions with Mr. Arthur Greenwood, Minister without Portfolio, particularly with respect to the trade union role in post-war reconstruction.[59] In support of the General Council, the congress expressed the "opinion that future world reconstruction should be in conformity with the standard of life aimed at by the Trade Union Movement." The congress also urged the General Council "to follow closely reconstruction programmes and policies as they develop with a view particularly to the control of financial interests and insuring speedy and continuous employment for all workers."[60]

Spokesmen for the largest unions at the congress in sponsoring this resolution made it clear that organized labor was agreed on a central theme—namely that it was essential for the trade unions to begin their preparations as soon as practicable if they were to act effectively to prevent a repetition of the experience of the inter-war years. They emphasized that they would regard as necessary the continued predominance of state control in the post-war economy and the treatment of questions of nationalization and the reorganization of industry as part of the general problem of reconstruction to achieve peacetime full employment. In addition to reaffirming its position for railway nationalization and instructing the General Council to draw up a plan for the coordination of transport after the war under public ownership, the TUC declared its support for the public control of land use.

Of particular significance was the decision of the TUC to urge the government to undertake a comprehensive survey of the related social services with a view to drawing up a plan for postwar implementation rather than to try to cope piecemeal with a national health scheme and other social welfare measures. Previous suggestions in the TUC for an integrated insurance system had lapsed during the 1930's for want of agreement among the trade unions over aspects of the operation of an insurance scheme as well as differences with the Labor Party over the principle of state family allowances, which the TUC opposed.

The Policies on Nationalized Insurance and Wartime Nationalization. Though its thinking on post-war planning was still in a preliminary stage, the TUC in 1942 defined its general policy as one of being "closely associated with the bodies responsible for detailed planning."[61] Through its representation on various governmental bodies, the TUC focused its attention on two post-war issues in particular: social services and education. Over the stiff opposition of the Insurance Workers' Federation, the TUC endorsed the proposals presented by the General Council to the Interdepartmental (Beveridge) Committee on Social Insurance and Allied Services. The committee had been established in accordance with the Coalition government's promise of the previous year. In presenting its views for a comprehensive overhaul and extension of national social service schemes, the TUC had recommended a state scheme which would satisfy the long-standing demand of the trade unions for the elimination of private companies from the whole field of social insurance and yet retain in some measure the traditional trade union association with the administration of such benefits. The TUC asserted: "The whole aim and purpose of social service is completely inconsistent with the furtherance of commercial interests and there should be no room for that in the new scheme. Bodies like Trade Unions, however, with their long and honourable tradition of service ought to be preserved so that the benefit of their experience and good will can be utilized in administration on behalf of the State."[62]

The TUC memorandum on social services also had urged adequate provision to safeguard the interests of all persons employed in existing schemes. Related to the demand by the TUC for a comprehensive system of social services was the reversal of its opposition to family allowances which it had opposed during the depression. The trade unions had argued that the allowance could serve as a government subsidy to wages which would undercut the unions' bargaining position in negotiations with employers. As it turned out eventually, the TUC also gave ground on the issue of trade union agency arrangements in the insurance scheme. It favored giving up trade union participation in the administration of sickness and unemployment benefits rather than see the extension of agency rights also to the industrial insurance companies under the proposed comprehensive scheme.[63]

While the trade unions were developing plans for post-war state schemes they nevertheless supported the Labor Party leadership in checking demands for wartime nationalization. This was part of the policy of shelving certain controversial issues which could jeopardize the unity of the Coalition government. Thus the TUC endorsed decisions by the National Council of Labor to examine each proposal for nationalization "on its merits as contributing to the successful prosecution of the war."[64] In effect this threw the weight of the trade union movement against a group of Labor Party "rebels" in the House of Commons who were demanding the "conscription of wealth," and in particular the immediate nationalization of mining, transport, and munitions, as a counterpart of the conscription of manpower for the war effort.

The Coalition government for its part had given assurances in Par

liament that it would not be timid or half-hearted in taking control
of any property to the extent that might be found necessary for the
full development of the war effort.[65] Previously, in support of this
policy, the National Council of Labor had prevailed upon the Miners'
Federation to accept the government's proposals for the comprehensive wartime control rather than the immediate nationalization of
the industry as a solution to the acute coal shortage.[66]

However, the decision not to press for wartime nationalization did
not weaken the basic trade union demand for nationalization of mining and transport as a necessary part of any plan for post-war reconstruction and for their incorporation as permanent features of
British economic life.[67] In addition to reaffirming its policies on mining and transport, the TUC went on record for national ownership
or control of land and water supply, and called upon the government
"for an immediate clear and comprehensive statement of planned
policies for post-war political, social and industrial reconstruction."[68]

Planning for Post-War Reconstruction—1943. With the tide of war
clearly changing in favor of the Allied Powers, the TUC entered into
the problems of post-war reconstruction and development as a principal activity. The TUC appointed six representatives to the (Re-
contruction) Joint Advisory Council set up by the government under
Sir William Jowitt who had taken over the responsibilities for look-
ing into post-war problems from Mr. Arthur Greenwood. Six other
members were chosen by the British Employers' Confederation and
the Federation of British Industries. In this context, the TUC drew
up a provisional list of long-range post-war reconstruction subjects
for examination. These included international labor relations, manpower redistribution and labor standards, economic controls, social
services, education, trade boards, and colonial development. With
respect to nationalization, the list mentioned specifically, but not
exclusively, coal and power, transport, the control or nationalization
of financial machinery, industrial assurance, and the utilization of
state-owned factories.[69]

At the 1943 congress the TUC adopted a comprehensive resolution
authorizing "the General Council to prepare and to circulate a general
plan for the post-war reconstruction of the industries of this country."[70] The plan was to deal specifically with the maintenance of
full employment; the principles of the public ownership and control
of industry; the extent of economic controls in the post-war period;
the nature of trade union responsibility in a planned economy; and

the adaptation of the plan by the trade unions to the industries with which they were associated.

Apart from this the TUC went on record for the complete nationalization after the war of the electricity supply industry, armaments, and the land. At the same time the congress endorsed the General Council's reaffirmation of policy that "the present time was inopportune to pursue the question of nationalization of industries contributing to the war effort."[71]

This congress also endorsed the first two major reconstruction reports commissioned by the government—the Beveridge Report on the social services,[72] and the white paper on "Educational Reconstruction."[73] With respect to the "nationalization" of social insurance, the TUC and the National Council of Labour were in general agreement with the recommendations of the Beveridge Report for a state scheme without the participation of private insurance companies. Nevertheless the scheme made provision for retaining friendly societies and trade unions to act as responsible agents for the administration of state sickness benefits, in conjunction with their own voluntary benefit schemes for members. The report also recommended the separation of death and other industrial insurance benefits from private insurance companies and their inclusion in the state scheme,—an objective the trade unions had been seeking since prior to World War I.

The congress in addition to demanding that the government initiate legislation immediately to implement the principles of the Beveridge Report[74] expressed its overwhelming approval of the government's white paper on education. This report was given parliamentary form in the Education Act of 1944, which the TUC regarded as a major step towards the "democratization" of educational opportunity.

The Interim Report on Post-War Reconstruction-1944. With the second front having been opened the previous June, and the defeat of Germany and Japan in sight, every major issue that came before the Blackpool congress was oriented towards post-war reconstruction. Compared with a quarter of a century earlier, the status, sense of responsibility, and influence in national affairs of the trade union movement were far greater. Delegates at the congress spoke with a marked consciousness of the practical possibilities of dealing with the inescapable industrial problems of the post-war period, and a recognition of the implications of their decisions with respect to the relationships of the trade union movement with both its Labor Party ally and with a prospective Labor government.

In addition to adopting a general program for meeting the economic challenge of post-war reconstruction, the congress dealt with major policy reports on trade union structure and closer unity; the government's white papers on "Social Insurance" and a "National Health Service"; the relationships between the public, i.e. private schools, and the state educational system; and the proposed organization of an international trade union conference which eventually led to the formation of the World Federation of Trade Unions. In the process the congress made general decisions on the role and priorities of nationalization in post-war reconstruction as well as on such specific items as "workers' control" and land nationalization.

The orientation of the post-war reconstruction policies of the TUC was indicated in a resolution which declared in part:

"Congress asserts that the continuation into the post-war period of Government controls, especially in regard to finance, raw materials, prices and the safeguarding of labour conditions, is imperatively needed to overcome the problems of the transition from war to a peace economy and urges the General Council to do everything possible to ensure that financial, commercial and industrial controls are not only maintained, but strengthened by increased direct participation of workpeople through their Trade Unions at all levels.

"Congress therefore welcomes the proposals which the General Council have put forward in their Interim Reconstruction Report, particularly the proposals for the immediate public ownership and control of the fuel and power and the transport industries and services."[75]

The TUC spelled out its views on the public ownership and control of industry as well as some broader aspects of its industrial and economic policy in its "Interim Report on Post-War Reconstruction."[76] The report arose out of the 1943 resolution instructing the General Council to draft a general plan on the subject. This the Council did in consultation with TUC affiliates and the Labor Party. In addition to the public control of industry, the report went into questions of finance and investment policy, prices and living standards, and the maintenance of full employment. The report collected and interpreted all the durable features of past trade union experience and thinking on the issue of the public ownership and control of industry, and combined them with the trade union assessment of what would be industrially possible and politically acceptable as minimum objectives in the public interest as an immediate program for post-war reconstruction.

This report, which was adopted as the considered policy of the British trade union movement defined the main objectives of the trade union movement as "The maintenance and improvement of wages, working conditions and living standards, the assurance to workpeople of adequate opportunities for suitable employment and the implementation of their right to share in the control of industry."[77]

"These objectives," the TUC declared, ". . . can only be adequately fulfilled within a system of public control. The alternative to public control is the increasing concentration of economic power in the hands of private persons and groups owing no responsibility to the community."[78]

Building on the 1932 report, "The Public Control and Regulation of Industry and Trade," which had set out the priority, degree and methods of public control, the 1944 report declared that "certain industries are of such vital importance . . . that their immediate transfer to public ownership is essential. They are notably the transport [railways, canals, road transport, coastal shipping, and internal airways], fuel and power [coal, gas, and electricity], and iron and steel industries." The report called particularly for the urgent nationalization of coal mining and railways for which "public opinion is most strongly prepared for the change to public ownership," even if "political opposition or legislative difficulties make it impossible to secure the complete transference of the whole of these industries [i.e. fuel and power, and transport] to public ownership."[79]

The report reaffirmed the general principles of public control developed since 1932. It stated that nationalized industries should be administered by public corporations. Members of governing boards should be appointed by the minister responsible for the industry in Parliament; and appointments should be made solely on merit; "but statutory provision should be made for adequate representation of the viewpoint of workpeople in the industry." Amplifying this point the report stated: "This could be secured by the selection of a number of the board's members from nominations submitted on behalf of the appropriate trade unions by the TUC. In addition there would be consultative councils at national, regional and sectional levels to advise the governing boards and their responsible officials on the formulation and administration of policy, and on these the trade unions would be represented by persons directly responsible to them."[80]

In private industry it was proposed that "workers' control" take the form of trade union representation equal to that of employers on industrial boards that might be set up to regulate an industry. These boards would have independent chairmen appointed by the government, and also trade union participation in consultative machinery at the plant level.[81]

Thus contrary to the terminology of doctrinaire socialist conceptions of class conflict, the "Interim Report" in effect defined "workers' control" as the achievement by workpeople of a voice in the conduct of economic affairs by collaborating with employers and the existing government rather than by attempting to gain control of industry and the state by following the strategy of economic warfare.

The principle of fair compensation was reaffirmed, payment to be preferably in various types of government-backed securities carrying a fixed interest rate. As in the 1932 report the basis of compensation recommended was "reasonable net maintainable revenue" i.e. compensation based on "the actual earnings over a period of years modified in the light of existing circumstances and the probability of the continuance of those earnings."[82]

In addition to the outright public ownership of specified industries, the report urged adequate control in the public interest over the utilization of land, water supply and other natural resources; over the supply of cash and credit, and the rate supply of capital investment; over the location of industry and general physical planning; and over foreign trade and investment.[83]

The report suggested criteria and methods for the regulation and direction of the nation's industrial sector. Short of complete public ownership the report suggested that the state could participate in the conduct of an industry by acquiring key sections of it or by "directive participation in particularly important companies." In other industries, which the report considered would require immediate direct public regulation and general planning, it was recommended that the aforementioned industrial boards could be established by the government to achieve unification, for example, as in cotton and woolen textiles, or to protect the public interest from the abuses of industrial monopolies.[84]

In conjunction with these views on the direct public control of specific industries the report called for the general control by the government over prices and standards of quality and over the level and direction of investments. It considered as "indispensable" that, "as a minimum the Governor of the Bank of England should be directly appointed by a Minister responsible for the policy of the Bank to Parliament, and a Coordinating Committee should be set up to exercise general guidance over the Joint State Banks."[85] Together with this the report proposed that the government prepare an annual "Manpower Budget" to estimate employment and determine public investment policies for the purpose of assuring employment to all available manpower.[86] Similarly, the report demanded the regulation and planning of foreign trade in a manner which would complement that of domestic trade. To this the report added: "We should do everything as a country to promote a policy of international expansion based upon increasing the productivity and standard of life of those great areas of the world which remain undeveloped economically."[87]

In addition to the basic policies of nationalization the congress dealt with specific situations. Thus it rejected a plan of the Union of Post Office Workers for reorganization of the post office so as to place it under the joint administration of the union and the state. The union and its predecessors in campaigning for the reform of employment practices in the Post Office for thirty years had been coupling long-standing grievances against the management of Britain's first nationalized undertaking with demands for "workers' control."

The TUC also tailored its policy of land nationalization to bring it into line with that of the Labor Party. It gave up its traditional demand for wholesale land nationalization in favor of limited measures as set out in the Uthwatt Report:

"State acquisition of all rights of development in undeveloped land, and the purchase, by compulsion if necessary, of all land at the time of its development."[88]

The TUC also expressed itself as being generally in favor of the nationalization of government-owned factories after the war as a measure to direct and assist post-war economic reconstruction.[89]

This congress warmly praised the government's plan for social insurance based on the Beveridge Report as "one of the greatest single advances ever made in this or any other country in the development of social insurance."[90] In the process, as indicated previously, the TUC accepted the decision of the Coalition government to abolish all agency arrangements for sickness and unemployment benefits—a traditional trade union function which had been recognized and provided for in the National Insurance system in 1911 by a Liberal Government. Benefits were to be administered directly by state departments. This decision went hand in hand with the displacement of a substantial business in private industrial insurance through the provision in the state-operated scheme of successor arrangements to workmen's compensation and burial benefits. The personnel of insurance schemes taken over or displaced were to be given employment priorities in the new state scheme.[91] Thereafter under the legislation of 1944-46 the entire statutory social and industrial insurance system was nationalized for direct state operation i.e. by government departments. In conjunction with the national insurance scheme, the TUC endorsed, with some qualifications, the government scheme for a national health service, i.e. for medical and related services.

With the climate of thinking permeated by the prospects for post-war reform the congress welcomed the comprehensive reforms of the Education Act of 1944. It also adopted a policy report on reorganization of trade union structure in the light of post-war problems. It urged the continuation of wartime labor-management joint production committees in the post-war period, and reaffirmed its policies of free collective bargaining as the basis of post-war labor management relations. It called for the establishment of the forty hour week "at the earliest practicable date,"[92] the extension of the powers of the trade boards, large scale public housing, and the repeal of the Trade Disputes and Trade Unions Act of 1927—something the TUC said it would regard as a general election issue.

The Transition Congress. By the time the Trades Union Congress convened again in the following year the war had ended, and the first Labor government having a clear majority over all other parties had taken office—with prominent trade unionists in some of the principal cabinet posts. Since the previous year the TUC had continued its work on policies which—as George Chester stated on behalf of the General Council—contained "as far as we could conceive them, practical answers to practical issues of post-war industrial policy on principles previously determined by Congress."[93]

Politically, the policies that had been developing in the trade union sphere had been embodied in an immediate short term program, "Let Us Face the Future," issued by the Labor Party in April as its general election platform. In it the Labor Party had outlined its plan for post-war reconstruction and an economy of peacetime full employment. It included the public ownership of fuel and power, inland transport, iron and steel, and the Bank of England; limited "land nationalization";[94] the public supervision of monopolies and cartels; a program of state aid and regulation of the export trade; and general economic and price control.

Bearing in mind the circumstances surrounding the new Labor

government and its commitments, and behaving with a conscious conviction that a new era had opened, the delegates to this congress sought to complete the program of post-war reconstruction basically set out the previous year. The congress expressed itself on important policies bearing on the nationalization of transport and the principles governing its financing; the nationalization of gas and coal; "workers' control"; the principles delineating the areas of public ownership and public control; the regulation of monopoly; and the role of fiscal and budget policy in guiding the economy.

While the policies adopted by the TUC on these issues carried great weight with the plans of the government which the TUC was pledged to support, it was made clear at the congress that there was by no means an identity of function or interest between the trade unions and the government. The trade union movement would reserve the right to act independently whenever it chose. This was stated by W. P. Allen in speaking on behalf of the General Council during a debate on workmen's compensation over which the TUC was having differences with the Labor government. "We are not anxious to create difficulties for the Government," he explained, "as you will have gathered from these proceedings, but the TUC is still not an appendage to any Government and must express its views."[95]

As with other policies, on questions of public ownership and control the views of the TUC and of the Labor government were fundamentally in accord. Where there were differences the prevailing spirit was one of working them out amicably with a minimum of embarrassment.

Thus the General Council did not present a coal scheme to the congress. As noted previously, the "Interim Report" had declared that the nationalization of coal was an imperative necessity even if for other reasons it might not be possible to carry out the nationalization of gas and electricity at the same time. In consideration of this, the TUC had begun to formulate a plan calling for the immediate nationalization of coal and the simultaneous establishment of at least a degree of public control over gas and electricity to assure the effective coordination of the three industries. However, in response to a request made in March 1945 by the newly-created National Union of Mineworkers (the successor to the Miners' Federation of Great Britain), a joint subcommittee of the TUC, the Labor Party and the Miners' Union had been set up to draft a scheme for the public operation of coal mining. Before the report had been completed, the general election had taken place, and the Labor government had followed with a pronouncement that it intended to nationalize coal mining without delay. The General Council informed the 1945 congress that the subcommittee, instead of publishing its report, had forwarded it directly to the Minister of Fuel and Power (Emmanuel Shinwell, who had formerly been chairman of the subcommittee) for his consideration in drafting the Coal Nationalization Act of 1946.[96]

As an extension of the "Interim Report" the TUC adopted a plan, "The Public Operation of Transport,"[97] for the public ownership and operation as a single complementary system of the seven separate transport services, i.e. railway, canal, road haulage, road passenger, ports and docks, coastwise shipping and internal airways. The report declared that the "National interest demands that the industry shall be administered with the object of providing the best possible services at the least real cost to the community. At the same time it must be organized so that it is capable of being deliberately operated as an instrument of national development, and of providing an improving standard of wages and conditions for the worker in the industry.[98]

The report took as its point of departure that "it is imperative that nothing shall be done to lessen the coordination achieved by British transport during the war."[99] It rejected the idea that a single efficient transport service in the public interest could be achieved through a private monopoly, and declared "the alternative is the complete coordination under public enterprise of all inland transport services."[100] As an immediate measure the report proposed that those sections of transport directly operated by or for the government during the war be placed under public ownership. The methods recommended for the takeover and the administration of transport by a National Transport Authority—a public corporation— were along the lines of policy set out and developed by the TUC in its 1932 program and afterwards, and which organized labor had come to accept as fundamental. In addition to the authority's immediate area of operating responsibilities it was to be responsible for seeing to it that its policies "harmonized with the government's general plans for the maintenance of full employment."[101]

As a result of a special study of the problems of compensation as applied to the purchase of British transport, the congress reaffirmed the policies worked out during the 1930's and restated in the "Interim Report."[102] It declared "That in general the most satisfactory basis of valuation was Reasonable Net Maintainable Revenue. Compensation would be based on the actual earnings over a period of years adjusted in the light of existing circumstances. Regard would also be paid to the probability of the continuance of these earnings. [This] would not, however, preclude the utilization of alternative methods in particular instances."[103]

Though the TUC had taken as its starting point "the desirability of establishing a degree of public control over the gas and electricity industries sufficient to ensure the effective coordination of the operations of the three industries,"[104] the congress nevertheless also went on record for the complete nationalization of the gas industry under a public corporation and its coordination with coal and electricity to form a composite service.[105] A memorandum to this effect had been submitted to the previously referred to Gas Industry (Heyworth) Committee. The proposals of the TUC followed the lines of public ownership as laid down in the 1930's and crystallized in the "Interim Report." The committee, which had been appointed to review the structure and organization of the gas industry to develop cheaper gas supplies, had recommended in December, 1945, the reorganization of the gas industry under public ownership.

Growing out of the "Interim Report" the TUC adopted a report on the broader question of "Trusts and Cartels." In addressing itself in this report to the problems of industrial and commercial monopoly —so basic to socialist concepts of public ownership—the TUC also presented justifications for the limitation of its nationalization objectives for the time being. Giving reasons for distinguishing between the purposes of public ownership and public control the report stated:

"The transfer of certain industries to public ownership has been considered by the TUC ultimately to be the only satisfactory policy for avoiding those dangers to the life and well-being of the community to which the growth of private monopoly gives rise. Nevertheless, for political and administrative reasons we have thought it necessary to concentrate upon securing the early socialization mainly of three groups of industries; fuel and power, inland transport and iron and steel. We have therefore proposed in the Interim Report various methods of public control for dealing with other industries whose ownership remains in private hands."[106]

The report conceded the abuses and disadvantages to the community of monopolistic practices. But in support of a general line of argument favoring the public control rather than the breaking up of monopolies, it contended that (a) industrial combination was an "inevitable development" of modern technology and "the competitive struggle itself,"[107] (b) trade unions had found that large undertakings were better employers and more favorably inclined towards stable collective bargaining relationships than small firms,[108] and (c) while there had been a need to prevent monopolistic abuses during the interwar years it had become clear also that where "the consequences of unrestrained competition were most severe and wasteful" some form of price regulation was necessary "to ensure that the industry . . . was in a position to pay decent wages out of its proceeds."[109]

In the light of the foregoing, the report concluded: "It would be undesirable generally to counteract the dangers arising from private monopoly in industrial organization by attempting to restore competitive conditions."[110]

Having ruled out the nationalization of all monopolistic enterprises for the time being, or a policy of breaking them up, the congress declared: "What is most urgently needed in relation to privately-owned industry is the establishment of proper machinery for the public supervision of combinations, associations and agreements which permit price management by private interests."[111]

For this purpose, in addition to a special government department and tribunal as permanent machinery to investigate and supervise private monopolies, the report suggested that the government employ a variety of measures to protect the public interest, e.g. the transfer to public ownership of an individual firm or a whole industry; the prohibition of specific trade practices of an obviously anti-social character; price control by government wholesaling or government production; or the promotion of cooperative or other forms of production in competition with established monopolies.

In addition to policies for the direct public control and ownership of industry, the TUC outlined its views on fiscal policy as a means of indirect control for purposes of economic planning. In a "Statement on Fiscal Policy"[112] the TUC stated categorically that "it is now clearly established that the Government and indeed the Government alone is able to control the general level of employment."[113] Consequently the TUC took the view that the government should use fiscal and budget policy for the wider purposes of sustaining adequate total demand. The government, said the TUC, should present and discuss its annual financial budget side by side with its estimates of the nation's income and outlay, and in conjunction with a "Manpower Budget" such as was proposed in the "Interim Report."

Apart from this the TUC advocated the use of fiscal and budget policy as an instrument to promote the equitable distribution of the national income and to provide incentives to productive efficiency.

Furthermore, the report declared that fiscal policy, as one part of the nation's economic policy must be treated in terms of its "full economic and social impact." Accordingly, "the Trades Union Congress as representative of the interests of workpeople, both as producers and consumers, should be consulted by the Government in determining fiscal policy."[114]

In various resolutions carried by the congress there were suggestions for planning or control in specific instances, e.g. distribution, scientific research, natural resources. But there were no new demands for nationalization. Rather there was a noticeable tendency to curb resolutions that could have been unnecessarily embarrassing to the Labor government. Thus, the congress shelved a resolution which largely repeated earlier demands that the government retain in peacetime the factories it had operated during the war. The Coalition government, of which the Labor Party had been a member, began earlier to lease the factories to private firms. Similarly, a move to retain aforementioned agency rights for trade unions under the National Insurance bill, then pending, was rejected. The TUC also decided not to go further into the question of land use and to leave the matter to the Labor Party. And when the Chemical Workers' Union pressed a resolution critical of the "Interim Report" in which "the old Conservative ideas on property are maintained," and demanded a final report which would "give a clear statement on the socialization of all basic industries,"[115] the resolution was referred to the General Council. The council reported to the next congress that it had rejected the criticism.[116]

The main effort of that trade union movement was directed at the complicated problems of the changeover from war to peace. But there was concern also with other issues of greater or lesser urgency than nationalization. The trade unions were occupied with the whole range of problems associated with demobilization, reemployment, and continued conscription. They had a vital interest in the pending legislation to repeal the Trade Disputes and Trade Unions Act, (1927). They were concerned with the intricacies of the social welfare legislation then in process. And they expressed themselves on long-standing issues such as the protection of minimum labor standards, equal pay for equal work, and the forty hour week. The first post-war congress authorized action by the General Council on a wide range of international labor and general foreign policy issues, too. However, the expression of British trade unionism on all these questions, as in the case of nationalization, represented a determination to assure the implementation of objectives long sought and promised rather than an enumeration of new demands.

IN SUMMARY

In the years between the National Strike and the end of World War II British trade unionism worked out with respect to nationalization its unique orientation combining radical conceptions with a strategy of moderation. For British labor as a whole this meant that in proposing changes in the basic property relations of the community it pressed its demands on those issues over which an accommodation could be reached within the democratic political process. For this purpose British labor rejected the application of rigidly partisan or doctrinaire formulae. Rather it chose to establish common ground with those outside its ranks who had their own reasons for accepting nationalization, either out of a broad concern over the nation's urgent economic and social problems, or because of a more direct interest in the welfare of a specific industry.

In the light of these considerations while British organized labor in its ideological approach to the nation's economic problems expressed itself in terms of creating a new society, it sought to relate its policies to objective conditions. Yet it attempted to avoid both sheer expediency and dogmatic extremes. Within this frame-work, its conception of "workers' control," for example, evolved into one which emphasized policies of furthering labor's sectional interests through the exercise of influence in the management of industry and the state.

In a comparable manner, organized labor's larger proposals for the nationalization of various industries and services were integrated into what was considered a practicable political program defined in terms of a planned economy and a welfare state. Its programs of economic reform and social and physical reconstruction were proposed to overcome glaring shortcomings in the existing system which to labor seemed incapable either of coping with chronic mass unemployment or of organizing production and distribution to end poverty.

The limitations labor imposed on its ambitions, together with the general national acceptance of the need for a real change in the British economic structure, served to lessen the resistance to nationalization outside organized labor. This also fitted the mood of a period when government intervention and planning in economic affairs was increasingly considered desirable, whether to protect the weak against the strong, or to rehabilitate the national economy; and when the temptation to project solutions into ultimate forms was exceedingly great. At the same time, labor, by a policy of political and industrial collaboration, established channels through which, by using the existing legal, economic, and social institutions, it was able to extend peacefully its ever-growing power until its full strength could be brought to bear at the end of World War II in support of the first government with a mandate to carry out its basic nationalization objectives.

The cumulative effects of World War I, the failure of milder remedies to cope with the sharpening dislocations in the economy during the inter-war years, the ramifications of World War II, and the necessities and spirit of reconstruction established the conditions for broad national agreement that the post-war period should bring with it a general reorganization of British economic and social life.

In this context the election of the Labor government in July 1945 marked the entry of organized labor into the days of its peacetime political and industrial power. However, organized labor achieved this position under circumstances in which the future development of its policies with respect to nationalization and other objectives traditionally associated with labor were likely to be conditioned initially by labor's enhanced responsibilities and the mellowing of the radical spirit gratified by reform and, in a more fundamental sense, the impact of powerful economic and political shifts in and out of Britain which were bound to put a new complexion on long evolving aims as well as require a reassessment by British labor of its ideological, political, and economic outlook.

IV

"THE PEACEFUL REVOLUTION"

In its first term the Attlee Labor government—the first Labor government with real power—carried through its promised nationlization measures on a scale indicative of a desire to break with the past.[1] To do this the government was in an unusually strong position. It had a heavy parliamentary majority and an electoral mandate. Its proposals fitted into an atmosphere of post-war reconstruction which the British public regarded as the government's responsibility. The TUC and the unions engaged in the industries affected pledged their efforts to make nationalization a success. And, notwithstanding the general opposition of the business community to the principle of nationalization, there existed a reservoir of cooperation among public-spirited businessmen willing to join in making public enterprises succeed.

In the main with variations allowing for different circumstances in each case, the Labor government followed the principles worked out by organized labor during the interplay of the pressures of the preceding fifteen years.[2]

Though total land nationalization had become an inactive issue, the Labor government dealt on a wholesale basis with the essential aspects of land development rights and the planned use of land with respect to specific national needs.[3] It completed the nationalization of statutory social insurance, also embracing benefits which had been an important part of the business of private insurance companies.[4] It nationalized the Bank of England,[5] coal,[6] civil aviation,[7] cable and wireless communications,[8] inland transport,[9] electricity,[10] gas,[11] and iron and steel.[12] It set up the Raw Cotton Commission and gave it exclusive power to perform the functions of importing and selling raw cotton in bulk, previously carried out by trading on the Liverpool Cotton Exchange.[13] The planning of the development of colonial resources was provided for in the Overseas Resources Development Act" under which the Colonial Development Corporation and Overseas Food Corporation were established as government-owned enterprises.

But events in the decade following the war profoundly changed the state of affairs which previously provided the trade union movement with ingredients to support its demands for nationalization. British society, free and orderly, made marked advances towards equality of opportunity and the abolition of unearned privilege. State action in the areas of social welfare, popular education, and justice removed some of the sharpest anxieties of the individual. Though the nation had serious economic difficulties, social security, full employment, and a remarkable increase in the real income of a majority of the people produced a standard of prosperity previously unknown in Britain. The popular understanding of economic problems and the degree of economic literacy of the nation as a whole had developed considerably. Mechanisms had been established to help maintain a national economic balance. The general acceptance that the government must play a decisive role in the economy had been built into the nation's fiscal and industrial structure by the fact of the government's continuing disposition of a large proportion of the national product.

In organized labor basic dissatisfaction with the organization of society virtually disappeared as an effective force. There was no lingering sense of betrayal of war aims on which suspicion could feed, as after World War I. But even more significant, British labor's election victory over an illustrious wartime leader, the implementation of its long developing objectives, and their absorption into the national way of life demonstrated to the British and to other socialist-minded labor movements throughout the world that the democratic way was a practicable alternative to Russian Bolshevism despite the latter's appeal at the close of World War II.

In the political sphere, unlike before the war, all parties accepted the premises of the welfare state and state responsibility for the condition of the economy. The Labor, Liberal, and Conservative parties were committed to the same general objectives relating to full employment with a rising standard of living, housing, social security, agriculture, education, and foreign policy—a situation to which the pressure for national unity heavily contributed under the constant tension of the cold war and economic crises.

The return of a Conservative government in 1951 confirmed that a new and wider area of government social and economic action had become commonly accepted, and that the nationalization of some key sectors of the British economy had ceased to be a political issue and had been absorbed into established national policy. As Prime Minister Sir Winston Churchill put it to the House of Commons: "It may sometimes be necessary for Governments to undo each other's work, but this should be an exception and not the rule. We are, of course, opposed, for instance, to nationalization of industry and, to a lesser extent, to the nationalization of services. We abhor the fallacy, for such it is, of nationalization far nationalization's sake. But where we are preserving it, as in the coal mines, the railways, air traffic, gas and electricity, we have done and are doing our utmost to make a success of it. . . . It is only where we believed that a measure of nationalization was a real hindrance to our island life that we have reversed the policy, although we are generally opposed to the principle."[15]

Thus the Conservative government did not carry out a sweeping doctrinaire denationalization of industry. It limited itself to policies of returning to private enterprise the control of the iron and steel industry[16] whose operations and economics had remained undisturbed by nationalization; reselling sections of road transport to private entrepreneurs;[17] setting aside the Labor government's scheme for nationalizing land development rights;[18] dissolving the Raw Cotton Commission and reopening the Liverpool Cotton Exchange for private trading;[19] and making changes in the administrative and legislative framework of other nationalized industries to improve their efficiency. This done, whatever the controversies over the performance of various nationalized enterprises, no effective public opinion for further denationalization remained.[20]

However, the Conservative government carried forward its policy of favoring private ownership in other ways. For example, whereas the Labor government had conceived and inaugurated the non-military development of atomic energy on a nationalized basis, the Conservative government in 1954 provided for the entry of commercial capital into the field to participate in its expansion. And in 1955 the Conservative government broke with broadcasting tradition when it decided to license commercial television to compete with the established nationalized television service.

In the wake of the sweeping alterations of the postwar decade much of the spirit of moral protest, the enthusiasm for planning that had existed at the end of the war, and the partisanship over nationalization abated. Without arguments being made for a laissez-faire economy, national thinking turned to questions of the limitations of planning in economic affairs, the effect of government intervention in introducing uneconomic distortions into industry, and the need to explore ideas for injecting into the economy more opportunities for competition and individual initiative. The dominant political and economic trends favored shifts from direct to indirect economic controls and concessions to a freer marketplace.

With respect to nationalized industries, the pressure for change was on the side of decentralization in management to allow fuller scope for initiative and responsibility, increased general accountability and responsiveness to the public and its needs, and a greater reliance on some of the more conventional commercial disciplines, such as profit and competition, in the conduct of public enterprise. Broadly, it may be said, that in economic affairs there was a trend away from the emphasis on stability and towards recognition of the necessity for change to compete in a rapidly changing world. The electorate indicated its leanings in turning away from the Labor Party towards Conservatives who, though by no means laissez-faire in outlook, favored greater reliance on individual incentive in formulating economic policy.

In the post-war period the British trade union movement also entered a new phase of development in which it was called upon to play a role very different from that in the past. Its new political and industrial power which was readily recognized in the community, unlike 25 years before, represented a change in the balance of forces in British society. Having succeeded in developing "workers' control" into a powerful general influence permeating the economy, the British trade union movement assumed responsibilities involving the future of the entire nation. It had to act with the consciousness of an "estate of the realm," apart from the fact that the scope of its interests meant that many of its actions cut more than one way.

Accordingly, for the first time in its history, the trade union movement had to exercise voluntary restraint in a peacetime economy because of its strength rather than because of the weakness of its bargaining position. This was particularly so in weighing the advantages and dangers that stemmed from full employment, the almost constant preponderance of inflationary pressures in the economy, and the problems of maintaining a state of precarious national economic stability. In these circumstances the nature of the economic crises in the 1950's called for a response from the trade unions quite the opposite of that to which they had been conditioned by the depression of the 1930's—namely to restrain rather to press at every opportunity their demands on the economy, and to think in terms of the increase rather than the redistribution of the national wealth.

The changed conditions of its environment required that British

labor rethink the situation as whole and its implications for the reconstruction of labor's internal and external relationships.   Many
ideas rooted in the industrial climate of the inter-war depression,
the defensive role of trade unionism, and a class alignment in politics
were thrown open to question.   Differences between the major parties
were narrower; the political partisanship of the trade union movement was blunted; and the influence of the trade union movement
in the affairs of state had grown far beyond its official political alliance.

With the disappearance of what might be termed "the fellowship
of penury," sympathy for organized labor as the underdog weakened,
and the attraction that "leftism" had had for "intellectuals" in the
1930's waned as well.   Moreover, the policies of economic levelling
began to lose support, not only among fixed income and professional
groups but also among skilled workers who saw their relative well-
being threatened and incentive deadened.   And the preponderance
of the forces of price inflation rather than those of deflation came
to be regarded by organized labor, as well as by other economic
interests in the community, as the main danger to full employment
and a sound economy.   What was more, a new generation had moved
onto the national scene.   Its memories of the 1930's were distant, and
its problems different from those of the depression generation.

RETHINKING LABOR POLICY

In a reconstructed environment the British trade union movement
had the task of adapting its form and function to its own decisive
role in British society, to the structure of the welfare state, and to
the framework of long-term solutions to the problems of post-war
Britain.   In this the trade union movement was faced with the dilem-
ma of reconciling its new level of national power and responsibility
with its traditional function of advancing the sectional interests of
the worker.

With respect to nationalization, the response of the trade union
movement to the experience in industries nationalized after 1945 was
not uniformly warm.   Whatever the professed ultimate ideals to the
advancement of which nationalization was expected to contribute,
nationalization was no longer confidently regarded as being particularly advantageous as a method of achieving trade union demands.
Rather, nationalization raised new questions and reservations in the
minds of trade unionists concerning the political and economic complications of dealing with a public monopoly, labor's voice and re-

sponsibility in publicly-owned industry, the operation of nationalized industries as instruments of public policy, and the special conditions these factors placed upon the conduct of labor-management relations. To this must be added the disappointment of many trade unionists whose anticipations as to what could be accomplished by nationalization had outrun reality.

More generally, the idea within organized labor that an economy based on private enterprise was unworkable lost its force. Many of the arguments advanced traditionally to justify nationalization either were no longer applicable or had not been supported by experience. The assumption which had colored the thinking of a generation of organized labor that industrial efficiency necessarily increased with size and the growth of state control became a matter of doubt, to say the least. The development of horizontal diversified commercial and industrial combinations raised issues different from those associated with the vertical industrial monopolies envisaged by socialist ideologists. And, what is more, the example of the distortion of the professed ideals of the Russian Bolshevik Revolution which coupled complete state ownership with political despotism served to undermine the faith in social ownership as a vital instrument for the emancipation of the workingman.

Allegations about the lack of social conscience and concern with the national interest of private enterprise were counterbalanced by fears about the growth of arbitrary state power. On the one hand, post-war experience had demonstrated how far social objectives could be achieved without expropriating private owners and without displacing the strong private motives which had beneficial economic effects. On the other hand the vesting of control of vital sections of the economy in what could become a managerial oligarchy with its own special interests and viewpoints roused apprehension as to the dangers this held for democracy and individual liberty.[21] Moreover, the sheer dimensions of the task of effecting the nationalization of large industries and operating them raised questions about the advisability of continuing on such a course, even apart from the paramount factor that the necessary measure of public support for further nationalization was lacking.

The Shift in the Trades Union Congress. The changing mood of organized labor was reflected in the TUC by a general watering down of its proposals for nationalization and the initiation of a rethinking of the whole question of social ownership. In 1944 the TUC had declared:

"The modern economic system bears little resemblance to the laisser-faire form of capitalism of a century ago. . . . Although the supporters of private enterprise still frequently plead their cases in the name of freedom, it is now abundantly clear that the liberty of the individual is most endangered by a system of unrestrained private enterprise.

"The choice before us is not between control or no control, but, in principle, between control by public authority responsible to the community, or control by private groups and persons owing final responsibility to themselves alone, and, in detail, between degrees of control and types of control."[22]

But six years later in its report on "The Public Control of Industry"[23] the TUC warned that, "public ownership should not be adopted simply for the sake of public ownership, but only as it is thought to be the best way of doing the job."[24] It concluded that "There is every indication that public ownership need not always take the form of nationalization of whole industries and there is important scope for selective and competitive public enterprises and further encouragement of Cooperation."[25]

In 1953 in its "Interim Report on Public Ownership,"[26] drafted by the General Council in consultation with the Labor Party, the TUC indicated that the British trade union movement had entered a new phase in its thinking on nationalization. The report, adopted by the annual congress after lengthy debate, reaffirmed the adherence of the TUC to the principle of public ownership and suggested some extensions, as in water supply and portions of the machine tool industry; but it committed itself to no new major measures of nationalization.[27] While the TUC stressed that it would give serious consideration to various proposals for public ownership or control, it significantly developed the theme that the trade union formula for nationalization as set out in the 1944 report had been shaped in an economic climate that no longer existed. It took the view that the time had come to assess the effectiveness of nationalization in terms of how well it had fulfilled the objectives hoped for in the past, and to apply the lessons of experience to future plans.

The spokesman for the General Council, Mr. C. J. Geddes (Union of Post Office Workers), in presenting the report pointed out that in considering the extension of nationalization as an industrial policy it had become necessary to weigh whether an industry transferred from private to public ownership was likely to remain so as a permanent feature of the national economy, since the question of denationalization, as well as nationalization, had become a reality.[28] On this point the report declared: "It would not be true today to say that public opinion is strongly prepared for the transfer of further industries to public ownership. Any proposals for the extension of this form of public control must therefore grow logically out of the experience of nationalization already gained, and out of the present needs of the community. Such proposals must not only be sound in themselves; they must be capable of attracting wide public support."[29]

The same congress endorsed a policy which "completely opposed" the government's denationalization proposals and rejected any idea of trade union participation on the Road Haulage Disposal Board or the Iron and Steel Holding and Realization Agency established to carry out the Conservative government's plans. However, it approved the General Council's negotiations with the government over labor questions involved in the process of denationalizing these industries. It also upheld the Council's actions which had led to the acceptance by three Council members of positions provided by the statute which had set up the Iron and Steel Board, the authority responsible for supervising the industry after denationalization.[30]

In the heated controversy surrounding the appointments, the General Council maintained that it was acting in accord with the fundamental function of trade unions—namely, that of representing the interests of workers in industry. It pointed out that agreement had been reached on the issue with the Labour Party, and that in any event "it is far better to exert our influence to control these things than to stand aside and have to take the consequences."[31]

At succeeding conferences while there were open differences as to the extension of nationalization, and criticism of the General Council's interpretation of the 1953 report, there was no reversal of the trend. A sharp controversy arose over the proposals for nationalization by the Confederation of Shipbuilding and Engineering Unions in its "Plan for Engineering." But the plan received the support neither of the TUC nor of the Labor Party. The strong feelings aroused among the opponents of the plan were dramatized in a widely publicized incident involving Arthur Deakin, general secretary of the Transport and General Workers' Union, the largest affiliate of the Labor Party and the TUC. Deakin attacked the plan as "a mumbo-jumbo of meaningless words and phrases," and then went on to warn: "The trade unions have done their utmost to create the measure of understanding with the political Labour Party that will enable us to go forth as a unified force. If you want to maintain that do not drive us into the position of falling out and breaking with the Party on such an issue as this."[32]

In 1955 the congress set aside for further consideration by the General Council a resolution urging the nationalization of "suitable sections of the engineering, chemical, and building and building materials industries."[33] James Campbell, general secretary of the National Union of Railwaymen, who on behalf of the General Council asked that the resolution not be passed, explained: "Our resolutions and our intentions must be translated into political action in order that by the coordinated effort of everybody in the movement we can devise what we consider to be a plan which will appeal to the electorate and avoid many of the mistakes of recent legislation for nationalization."[34]

The General Council the following year was supported by the congress when it emphasized the "thorough investigation of particular industries was essential," and summarized the general policy of the TUC as applied to engineering as follows: "The acceptance by the TUC of the principle of public ownership and control, . . . did not imply that, in their consideration of a particular industry, the General Council were bound to start from the assumption that some way must be found of bringing it immediately into public ownership or that it was necessary to extend to it immediately any form of control additional to those exercised over industry generally by the Government [as] . . . was indeed accepted in the Confederation's own "Plan for Engineering."[35]

By the time of the 1957 congress, the post-war trend in trade union policy had been given a large measure of expression in the restatement of Labor Party policy on public ownership (discussed below) issued the previous July for the consideration and endorsement of the October party conference. Notwithstanding some very sharp direct and implicit criticisms at the congress that the party's view of the future role of public ownership was a betrayal of the socialist tradition in the interests of political expediency, TUC policy remained basically consistent with that of previous years and in harmony with that of the Labor Party. The congress endorsed an agreement that the General Council had arrived at with the Labor Party and the Confederation of Shipbuilding and Engineering unions favoring the nationalization of sections of the machine tool industry, and it reaffirmed its support generally for the extension of nationalization as an instrument of labor policy. But it made no new specific commitments for public ownership and it otherwise pledged itself to work "in conjunction with the political wing of the movement, in shaping Labour's next General Election programs."[36]

The ninetieth congress in the following year confirmed, in effect, this restricted approach to nationalization. This, despite charges by more doctrinaire critics that labor's nationalization policy, as it stood, now actually limited further nationalization to inefficient industries and granted immunity from nationalization to successful private enterprise. The congress reaffirmed its tradition of nationalization of the basic industries as well as previous commitments to nationalize key sections of the machine tool industry, and to renationalize iron and steel and road transport. Sentiments for a larger voice for labor on the boards of nationalized industries were expressed in a decision pledging the TUC to take up with a future Labor government the question of making appointments only from among those sympathetic to nationalization, and to draw more appointees from the trade union movement. But the Congress set aside resolutions to extend nationalization to the construction and tobacco industries.

In expressing the opposition of the General Council particularly to placing tobacco on a "shopping list" of problem industries to be nationalized, Mr. J. A. Birch (Distributive and Allied Workers' Union) declared that no basic argument for the nationalization of the industry had been made. He emphasized that the tendency towards monopoly was only one of several criteria which labor policy applies in determining the need for nationalization: "We have said in Congress time and again that monopoly is one of the criteria for nationalization, but we have also said that there are other criteria, including the nature of the service provided by the industry, with particular reference to the basic services on which the community depends, the need to develop an industry rapidly to enable us to obtain economic independence and security, and the need to improve organization and methods which are required in an industry if living standards are to be raised. In none of these other categories does the tobacco industry fall."[37]

The Shift in the Labor Party. Labor Party policy in the postwar years reflected a kindred trend to that of the TUC. In 1946 Prime Minister Attlee, in reviewing his first year in office, had told the Labor Party conference:

"We . . . are resolved to carry out as rapidly and as energetically as we can the distinctive side of Labour's programme: our socialist policy, our policy of nationalization.

"These [programs of nationalization] are not theoretical trimmings. They are an essential part of a planned economy that we are introducing into this country. They are designed to help in promoting full employment, economic prosperity and justice for all. . . . They are the embodiment of our socialist principle of placing the welfare of the nation before that of any section and of dealing with every problem in a practical and businesslike way."[38]

The Attlee Labor government, as previously described, enacted the program pledged for its first term, but it otherwise displayed a tendency to emphasize the consolidation rather than the extension of public ownership. Afterwards, out of office, though the Labor Party promised to renationalize iron and steel and road haulage on becoming the government again, it made no strong argument for further nationalization on a comparable scale. Rather, such items as the nationalization of industrial insurance, sugar refining, cement and chemical manufacture disappeared from its agenda of active demands. And, in contrast to its previous proposals for the creation of state monopolies, the Labor Party began to shift its emphasis to public ownership through piecemeal acquisition, and the operation of public enterprise on a competitive basis with private enterprise in a mixed economy.

The Labor Party also arrived at very much the same conclusions as the TUC about the need for rethinking the whole question of nationalization. Thus the Labor Party conference of 1955, while "reaffirming its belief in the common ownership of production and distribution," instructed the National Executive Committee to "prepare a comprehensive report on the set up of the present nationalized industries" which ". . . could be used as a guide to the future extension of public ownership of industry."[39]

Speaking in support of the resolution on behalf of the National Executive Committee, Hugh Gaitskell, while reiterating his belief in the idea of public ownership as a lever of economic policy, declared: "I would venture to say this, that I think the time has come when we must look at the place of nationalization and public ownership in relation to the whole strategy of democratic socialism."[40] While defending the nationalization measures taken by the Labor government after 1945, Gaitskell summed up the political problem this way: "Why was it that the people of this country were prepared to accept our nationalization proposals in 1945, but not to accept them in 1950, 1951, or 1955? I would say in all seriousness that this was not because in 1945 we had converted a majority of the electors to a belief in our fundamental principle. It was not, and we delude ourselves if we think it was. It was because we had convinced them that in these particular industries nationalization was the right course. . . . When we come to 1950, 1951, and 1955 we have got to admit we failed in those years to get across our nationalization proposals to the people. . . . I do not think there is very much doubt that we probably lost rather than gained votes from them. These are unpleasant things but we must face them."[41]

It was this conference which endorsed a proposal by the National Executive Committee for the re-examination of party policy by ten study groups which would prepare a series of policy reports to be discussed at the three succeeding annual conferences. The 1956 Labor Party conference adopted statements on "Personal Freedom," "Homes for the Future," "Towards Equality," and "Colonial Policy." The 1957 conference adopted reports detailing a pension scheme for the future—"National Superannuation"[42]—and promised to submit full policy statements to the next conference on the atomic and automative age, agriculture and the land, and central planning and control.

With respect to public ownership, apart from reaffirming its previous commitments on the public ownership of water supply and sections of machine tools, the 1957 conference after extensive discussion and criticism adopted by a four to one majority two basic reports drafted in consultation with the TUC—"Public Enterprise," and "Industry and Society."[43] The former assessed from the point of view of British organized labor the performance in the post-war decade of industries the Labor government had nationalized; the latter presented an analysis of the future of public ownership and outlined future policy.

According to the report on "Public Enterprise," the record of the nationalized industries provided "strong practical justification of Labour's policy of public ownership"[44] notwithstanding the handicaps of the post-war economic crises and the political controversy that surrounded the industries concerned. The report reviewed criticisms of organization, management, consumer and labor relations, and public accountability facing these industries, as well as questions of economic and financial policy for which it offered some suggestions for improvement. But on the whole it dismissed "categorically" criticism even of "convinced socialists" as regards the relationships of the nationalized industries with Parliament, with their employees and with consumers as "based for the most part on misunderstanding."[45] It concluded that "the foundations laid during the last ten

years are sound, and that the legislative framework within which
the Boards operate will enable them to discharge faithfully and well
the important tasks which were laid upon them.[46]

The "modified" approach to public ownership as set forth in "Industry and Society" was by way of recognition that "major changes
have taken place during recent decades in the structure of industry
and in the degree of state influence over the economy."[47] The report
did not rule out further nationalization. But it shifted the basic discussion of nationalization from the predominant pre-war considerations of the benefits and abuses of monopoly, the depressed aspects
of British industry, and the redistribution of wealth. It addressed
itself rather to the problems of introducing appropriate forms of
public accountability and control over the dominant firms in industry,
and of securing for the community an "increasing share of the fruits
of industrial expansion"[48] in a mixed economy capable of being guided
in a significant degree by government policy.

The report compared the pre-war aims of organized labor with
their fulfillment in the new post-war economic environment to which
labor's own programs had contributed so substantially. It noted the
evolution of private industry since the Labor Party had adopted its
socialist objective in 1918, particularly with respect to the role of large
firms which, while not necessarily monopolies in a doctrinaire socialist definition, exercised a leading influence in the economy because
of their size, stability and distinctive organizational character.

Narrowing down its analysis, the report estimated that some five-
hundred of the largest corporations probably accounted for nearly
half the total profits of private industry and eighty percent of the
total capital appreciation of public stock equities. These firms, according to the report had become main centers of post-war economic
growth. The report pointed to the divergence of interest, incentive
and power as between the dispersed stockholders and the increasingly independent professional management. It noted the automony
over capital investment large companies enjoy through self-financing.
And it concluded that a new form of business organization had
emerged.

The large public corporation, as distinct from the small company,
the report observed, had assumed characteristics resembling a public
institution with a life and purpose of its own. The large corporation was progressively dwarfing the individual investor's role. In
large part this had been due to egalitarian policies of high progressive
taxation and death duties as well as general industrial expansion.

These policies had encouraged the retention and reinvestment of earnings by corporations so that profits to equity shareholders had taken the form of capital gains rather than distributed dividends. In these circumstances shareholders were getting benefits without assuming for the most part the traditional capitalistic functions of risk taking, management and supplying the main capital for investment. What was more the shareholders in the large firms remained a continuing cause of perpetuating inequalities of wealth, for shareholders were mainly among the wealthier sections of the community.[49]

In sum, the report argued that the large firm was related to the classic model of private monopoly which socialists have traditionally attacked, and was the creature of historical forces. Its size was substantially determined by economic and technological developments. Its stability was underwritten by the commitments to full employment and industrial expansion of the modern welfare state as well as its own resources. Its professional management, which was a product of modern business necessity, wielded vast industrial powers independently of its owners or the public interest, which it might or might not be serving well. Its new financial structure was the result of the substitution of institutional wealth for individual wealth.

Drawing a parallel between the gains in equity values ascribable to the policies of the welfare state to underwrite prosperity and full employment in industry, and past socialist arguments about socially-created increments in land values, the report claimed "the community should have the opportunity of participation in the almost automatic capital gains industry."[50] For this, quite apart from questions as to the assumption of managerial control by the state in given instances, the report recommended the systematic acquisition of equity shares by the state by various means, e.g. by the acceptance of equity shares in payment of death duties, or through investments in industrial shares by the National Superannuation Fund to protect the future value of benefits under the proposals in the Labor Party's new pension policy.[51]

However, the report viewed the extension of public ownership as one of several alternative methods of economic control, and distinguished between partial public ownership and the nationalization of entire industries under single control. Pointing out (in contradiction to doctrinaire socialist theory and the line of thought of the 1944 TUC "Interim Report") that the advantages of unified control "will frequently be outweighed by the advantages of autonomy and competition," the report observed that, "we must adapt the forms of public ownership to meet the particular problems involved."[52] In place of drawing up a "shopping list" of industries to be nationalized as was the practice in the past, the report took this position:

"In recent years inquiries into the problems and organization of several other industries have been undertaken by the Labor Party, by the TUC, and by other groups in the Labor Movement. Although much useful spade work has been done many of the facts upon which judgment must be based are simply not available to an Opposition Party; and—an additional complication in a period of great industrial development—the facts themselves can rapidly change.

"That is why we emphasize the need for the next Labor Government to supplement such research as has been done by a new series of official enquiries before decisions are taken."[53]

While not closing the door on nationalization in order to reorganize and rationalize industries as state monopolies, the report emphasized that its proposals for public ownership were designed to meet a different set of problems: "Thus it may be that public ownership of a single firm will suffice to break a production bottleneck or restore competition in a monopolized industry. It may be that new industries, like atomic energy, can be pioneered from the start under public ownership. It may be that public participation in a private firm can be secured through State investment in it."[54]

As for the special problems posed by the large firms, the report declared as a general policy that in the interests of assuring their public accountability "a new and closer relationship between the large firms and the State will be required."[55]

Supplementary to this review of the economic power of large firms the report urged that their exercise of social power should also be reviewed to eliminate privileges of status and social advantage that had grown up, for example, as part of the "standard of working"[56] of executives.

Summing up its argument in terms of the overall labor objective of greater equality the report claimed, that if private shareholders ceased to exist, the large companies would not be harmed in the slightest; that while in a substantial section of industry "private ownership has ceased to be necessary . . . it is still a major bulwark of inequality of wealth in our society;" and that "a transfer [from private to public ownership] would contribute powerfully towards a better distribution of wealth."[57]

While reaffirming many traditional precepts, the Labor Party, which had consulted the General Council in working out its reports on public ownership, had in effect recast labor's policy. It had shifted the emphasis from that of taking over entire industries designated as essential for planning the production and distribution of economic wealth to that of establishing various degrees of public ownership in the corporate structure. This was to be done after a thorough study of objective conditions in each case.[58]

This modernized formulation of the purposes and methods of state penetration into an economy that would remain mixed meant that British labor did not contemplate the imminent extension of public ownership to new industries,[59] and no longer considered nationalization to be as important a tool of economic policy as socialists traditionally had believed. Therefore organized labor did not think it suitable to pledge a future Labor government to any firm commitments in this respect. The flexibility of interpretation to which this formulation of public ownership lent itself was in accordance with the pragmatic attitude that British organized labor, and especially the British trade union movement, had taken historically towards the idea of nationalization. This also was suited to a political situation where any proposal for nationalization had to be clearly justified as economically necessary on its merits and where admission of sheer doctrinaire inspiration would be an electoral liability. As stated by British labor's political leader, Hugh Gaitskell, to the 1957 Labor Party conference: "We understand from our point of view what you may call the long-run case for nationalization. But the millions of electors we have to convince, including many millions of Labour supporters, are not quite so well educated in socialism as that, and they will not be satisfied if, when they ask, 'Why are you proposing to take over this industry?' you simply reply, 'Because that is socialism.' They want to know what the specific reasons are for nationalizing . . . this particular industry."[60]

The fifty-seventh party conference adopted the three remaining studies on the "rethinking" of basic policies initiated in 1955 in conjunction with the TUC. It, too, evidenced the tendency to minimize the theme of nationalization. The party restated its agricultural policy in "Prosper the Plough"[61] substantially in terms of an overall government program for planned agricultural expansion and various measures to aid farmers; but it rejected an amending resolution which reaffirmed labor's historical demand for the nationalization of the land as the solution to the problems of agriculture. Tom Williams, who had been the Minister of Agriculture responsible for shaping and implementing the basic agricultural reform policies set out by the

Attlee Labor government in the 1947 Agriculture Act, summed up:

"Nationalization may or may not be good. . . . There has never been a detailed examination of all its implications either as to cost, the colossal administration required, or its political implications. I want to say to those who theoretically feel it might be good, that they had better place before Conference at some time in some form their detailed proposals for carrying out the policy they want to impose upon the National Executive; but in any case from the viewpoint of *Prosper the Plough* land nationalization has little or no relation to agricultural policy as such. I do not think it would influence the production of one ton either more or less, and to that extent it ought not to form part of *Prosper the Plough*. I am convinced that anything in the nature of an unconsidered land nationalization proposal would not only wreck our chances for the next election but perhaps keep us in the political wilderness for a very long time."[62]

In "Learning to Live,"[63] the Labor Party presented proposals for extensive improvements in education, but rejected as unrealistic and impractical the view that the influential public, (i.e. private schools —symbols of class privilege—and state-assisted fee-paying private schools, be abolished or taken over by the government and integrated into a national system of free education. Rather, the Labor Party's policy left the private schools relatively untouched and emphasized that the democratization of educational opportunity should come through the expansion and improvement of the quality of existing free educational facilities rather than through the abolition of private schools.

In "Plan for Progress,"[64] the Labor Party outlined its ideas for the controlled expansion of the economy through central planning. This, it was claimed, would ensure both economic stability and full employment. As for the use of nationalization to deal with certain industrial situations in the national interest, the Labor Party reiterated: "We do not approach such problems in any doctrinaire spirit. In the steel and road haulage industries, public ownership will be reintroduced because the case for national ownership is, on its merits, overwhelming. In other industries we shall take whatever action is shown to be necessary."[65]

Moreover, in summarizing labor's views on the methods of social planning, "Plan for Progress" made it quite clear that labor's policy of controlled economic expansion did not necessarily consider nationalization as the most desirable method for achieving its goal: "There is no single type of control which offers a panacea to all our problems. Budgetary and monetary policies, direct controls and public ownership, persuasion and publicity, are all techniques we shall use with equal readiness whenever appropriate. What matters is not so much the techniques themselves, but the will to make them effective. It is essential to have a Government that will not be deterred, either by fear of vested interests or by some ideological mind barrier, from doing what is in the national interest."[66]

In its program for the next Parliament issued as labor's platform for the 1959 general elections,[67] the Labor Party's public ownership commitments were limited to the reaffirmation of past policies, but included no additions. Emphasis was placed on public control rather than ownership as the device for making the dominant firms of the economy publicly accountable. Symbolic of the historical as well as contemporary trend was the deliberate omission of labor's first nationalization objective—that of land—three quarters of a century after it first had appeared in the policies of the British Trades Union Congress.

With an unspoken consciousness of nationalization as an electoral burden, the Labor Party generally avoided discussion of the issue during the campaign to the degree practicable. Nevertheless, nationalization, even in a comparatively tacit role, retained its significance as a characteristic of British labor policy, and contributed to labor's decisive and third successive election defeat. Other issues of foreign and domestic affairs held the center of public attention during the campaign debates. But in the post-election self-examination the heated controversies within organized labor once again centered on the nature of British labor's association with nationalization as it concerned labor's whole approach to the social and economic problems of the second half of the twentieth century.

V

NATIONALIZATION AND TRADE UNIONISM
IN A DEMOCRATIC SOCIETY

The change in the outlook of British trade unionism in the post-war reconstruction decade, so significant in terms of the contemporary policies of organized labor, is in accord with the main stream of British trade union tradition. The character of this tradition has been reflected probably more completely in the formulation of nationalization than through any other single issue.

Nationalization as an aspect of British labor policy emerged from World War II in every detail of its philosophy and method fitted to the laws and customs of a democratic society and the practical considerations of protecting the rights and advancing the interests of trade unionists. Thus, though frequently vaguely conceived in terms of social and economic radicalism focussed on the emancipation of labor, nationalization was regarded by British trade unionism as a medium for orderly, purposeful change. It was the end product of intense and often bitter debate in the labor movement rather than the result of a victory by a compact, like-minded group which had successfully propagated a dogma of social advance. And just as British labor was non-doctrinaire with respect to nationalization, it was non-doctrinaire in its attitude towards private enterprise.

Throughout this process, British trade unionism characteristically rejected extremist analyses of society as a structure kept essentially inflexible by entrenched interests. It preferred the path of seeking to increase social and economic mobility using the existing political machinery, and it accepted as basic that in a democracy there can only be as much of anything as the electorate will permit. It attached special significance to the overlapping and mutual effects of political, economic and social interests, but it rejected theories which assumed the identity of these interests; and it differentiated among the functions of political, industrial, and social organization. Accordingly, the British trade union movement could differ with other groups in the community in some respects and retain a basis for collaboration in other respects.

British trade unionism made its appeal in terms of community over sectional interest. In doing so it accommodated itself to the complications and subleties of satisfying individual situations and gathering maximum non-trade union support for general labor objectives. Also, while British trade unionism pressed for state intervention against private business interests, its thinking was tempered by a consciousness of the danger of endowing the government with powers unbalanced by other forces in the community. It did not regard state action as the only means of social progress, and it demanded for itself full freedom from state control. In sum, British trade unionism treated revolution as a contradiction of evolution. It preferred to build on existing democratic institutions rather than detour by experimentation with theories which claimed that the path to true democracy lay through class extermination and political dictatorship.

As has been described, since the founding of the TUC, nationalization as a trade union demand for governmental action to curb private interests has fallen into various frames of reference. After an initial period of indifference, the TUC associated nationalization with the need to reform anachronistic institutions of land ownership to suit modern industrialized society. Thereafter nationalization became associated with the movement which feared the growth and concentration of economic power as a threat to the popular will and good. During the inter-war years nationalization was tied to the basic problems of unemployment and depression. During World War II it became a key measure in labor's program for sweeping post-war reform and reconstruction. After the war, along with the realization of its program, British labor found itself in the new environment of a welfare state in which it enjoyed unprecedented influence. Thus the British trade union movement had arrived at another period of transition in its thinking.

This does not mean British labor is ready to turn its back on nationalization. On the contrary the principle of nationalization, though undergoing redefinition, remains officially favored in labor policy. Acceptance of the policy of "piecemeal" public ownership is a continuation of the policy of state participation in private enterprise spelled out by labor in its basic reports of the 1930's and recast in the 1940's. Moreover, the idea that socialistic ownership represents a higher economic and social form than commercial enterprise remains a considerable force in labor thinking. Yet the TUC, for instance, in terms of its Standing Orders, can claim that with

minor exceptions, e.g. minerals, its nationalization objectives have
been fulfilled.   Therefore it can with reason prefer at this stage to
examine the achievements and weaknesses of nationalization, and
more broadly the whole question of the relationship between industry and the state.

In this context, as in the past, the conception and execution of
nationalization remains subject to the tests of politics, economics,
trade unionism, ideology, and the dominant contemporary problems
of the country—but this time in the light of conflicting assessments
of the experience with nationalization which organized labor has
been instrumental in bringing about.   This also means that the
Labor Party, of which the trade unions form the base, has to reflect
on some of its objectives and its interpretations of social change—
including the purposes and possible alternatives to nationalization
in the conceptions of British socialism.   The Labor Party also has to
think through where it wants to go next as a party of reform.

Nevertheless it has become clear already that in the re-thinking
by British organized labor about policy there has been a distinct decline in the importance attributed to nationalization.   This is so at
least to the extent of deciding as to what part, if any, nationalization should play in future programs of legislation; apart from the
appearance of a genuine uncertainty about some other methods and
objectives of British socialism.   Thus, the challenge to the principle
of nationalization, however indirect, is significant, and involves a
realignment of labor policies generally.   Such a situation precludes
the vigorous unified labor support for further nationalization proposals necessary to make a simple clear-cut case to impress the
electorate.

British labor's re-evaluation of its ideas may be regarded as a new
stage in the development of the social idealism, the feeling of communal fellowship, and the adherence to certain ethical principles
which from the beginning have been so influential in shaping labor's
assessment of society and its problems.   This process of re-thinking
is in complete accord with British labor's traditional approach; that
is, of treating problems of the individual's welfare empirically and
directly, and of regarding the organization of human affairs in terms
of changing values and relationships rather than in terms of the single-
minded pusuit of a static ideal of society.

REFERENCES

CHAPTER I

1. Though socialist elements were active and influential in bringing about sponsorship of the LRC after a bitter fifteen year debate within the TUC over independent labor representation, they were also somewhat circumspect so as not to alienate possible support in the trade unions. For example, this consideration caused the word "socialist" to be left out of the name of the Independent Labor Party (ILP) when it was formed in 1893, although the ILP had adopted a socialist objective. Ben Tillett, the dockers' secretary and a self-proclaimed socialist, was cheered at the founding conference of the ILP when he declared, "For real, vital effective work there was not a Socialist party in the whole world who could show such effective organization as these men [Tory trade union leaders] could. . . . If the Labor Party [i.e., the ILP] was to be called a Socialist Labor Party I would repudiate it." (See *Independent Labor Party, Report of the First General Conference, Bradford, 14th January, 1893, p. 3.*

2. *TUC Annual Report, 1882,* pp. 35-36.

3. *TUC Annual Report, 1886,* p. 41.

4. *TUC Annual Report, 1894,* p. 219.

5. *TUC Annual Report, 1895,* p. 52.

6. Although the Labor Party regularly introduced nationalization bills in Parliament as requested at the annual trades union congresses, it is of interest that at the 1906 congress Will Thorne, a leader among trade union socialists, apologized to a critic that union business had kept him from the House of Commons the day the nationalization bill had come up on the calendar, and no other Labour M.P. had known enough about it to take his place and speak for the bill (*TUC Annual Report, 1906,* p. 158). In 1907 nationalization was lost in a congress dominated by the miners' eight-hours bill and the first threatened national rail strike organized by the all-grades movement. In 1908 the TUC passed a general nationalization resolution covering land, minerals, mines, canals, and railways.

7. See Winston S. Churchill, *Liberalism and the Social Problem* (London: Hodder and Stoughton, 1909), pp. 80-81.

8. In this respect, the election in 1912 of Robert Smillie as president of the Miners' Federation, the first socialist ever to hold that position, was significant. Smillie was a spirited advocate of mining nationalizaton, and the miners accounted for more than a quarter of the membership of the TUC. He was materially assisted by a similar trend in other TUC affiliates, notably the railwaymen and other transport unions.

9. As President of the Board of Trade, Winston Churchill was the responsible minister for the Port of London Authority. He defended provisions for labor representation on the port authority on the grounds that, "Although it is an interest of a particular class, that class is so interwoven that it cannot be dismissed as wholly sectional; it is a human, moral, and sectional interest of a large and responsible character." (Quoted in Lincoln Gordon, *The Public Corporation in Great Britain,* London: Oxford University Press, 1938, p. 29.)

10. With advantages to them outweighing objections, the trade unions accepted the contributory health and unemployment insurance schemes based on
the Liberal principle of compulsory self-help in opposition to the socialist principle that the state must guarantee its citizens the "right to work" or otherwise
provide maintenance as a social charge against the state. The debates and parliamentary tactics surrounding passage of the bill led to considerable controversy
within the Labor Party between trade unionists and determined advocates of
socialist principles. (See G. D. H. Cole, *A Short History of the British Working
Class Movement*, 1787-1947 [London: George Allen and Unwin, 1948], p. 309).
Between 1910 and 1913 trade union membership increased almost 70%, from
2,555,000 to 4,135,000. TUC membership rose from 1,648,000 to 2,232,000. The
most substantial gains were among miners, general workers, clerical employees,
railwaymen and other transport workers.

11. *TUC Annual Report, 1911,* p. 163.

12. *TUC Annual Report, 1910,* p. 191.

13. *TUC Annual Report, 1913,* p. 198.

14. Sidney and Beatrice Webb—*History of Trade Unionism* Revised Edition,
extended to 1920 (London: Longmans, Green & Co., 1920), p. 661.

15. *TUC Annual Report, 1915,* p. 78. The railway unions at this time also
were seeking representation (without success) on the Railway Executive Committee established by the Government to run the railways taken over at the outbreak of the war. The committee consisted of the managers of the principal
railway companies under the chairmanship of the President of the Board of Trade.

16. *Ibid.,* p. 288.

17. *TUC Annual Report, 1916,* p. 398.

18. *Ibid.,* p. 250-251.

19. *Ibid.,* p. 74.

20. *TUC Annual Report, 1917,* p. 351.

21. In opposing the resolution for insurance nationalization, a delegate from
the Insurance Workers' Union, declared, "It must not be assumed either that the
whole of the insurance agents of the country are in favor of the nationalization
of the industry . . . However badly we may be treated by the companies at the
present time there is no guarantee that we should not be treated far worse by
the Government under any scheme of nationalization. The probability is, the
first effect of nationalization would be to throw at least one-half of the insurance
agents upon the scrap heap." (*TUC Annual Report, 1918,* pp. 274-275.)

22. *Ibid.,* p. 177.

23. *Ibid.,* p. 176. Robert Smillie explained his union's position at the end of
the war this way: "The syndicalist idea of miners working, managing and owning
the mines has not a very deep hold on the miners of this country. They fully
expect, if the mines are owned and controlled by the State, that the workmen
will have a considerable voice in the management, in view of the fact that they
have more than livelihood at stake. Their safety of life and limb justifies the claim
that they shall be represented in the management." (Paul U. Kellogg and Arthur
Gleason. *British Labor and the War,* New York: Boni and Liveright, 1919,
p. 176.)

24. The Labor Party's socialist objective read: "To secure for the producers
by hand or by brain the full fruits of their industry, and the most equitable distribution thereof that may be possible, upon the basis of the common ownership

of the means of production, and the best obtainable system of popular administration and control of each industry and service." (*Labor Party Annual Report, 1918,* Seventeenth Annual Conference Jan.-Feb., 1918, Appendix 1, p. 140.) Edward R. Pease, for 25 years the secretary of the Fabian Society, described this as an "admirable definition of collectivist socialism as understood by the Fabian Society" (Edward R. Pease, *History of the Fabian Society.* London: Allen and Unwin, 1925, p. 264).

25. Labor Party, *Labor and the New Social Order. A Report on Reconstruction.* Labor Party London, 1918.

26. Kellogg and Gleason, *op cit.*, p. 373.

27. *Ibid.*

28. *Ibid.*, p. 374.

29. *Ibid.*, p. 383.

30. *Labor Party Annual Report* (Eighteenth Conference, June 1918) 1918, p. 44.

CHAPTER II

1. In the case of airways for example, Lord Weir, the Secretary of State, Royal Air Force stated "that though in his opinion the state should play a large part in the development of aviation, he does not contemplate the nationalization of the whole industry as desirable in the interests of the State." (*TUC Annual Report, 1919,* p. 89).

2. See Arthur C. Pigou, *Aspects of British Economic History, 1918-1925.* London: Macmillan Co., 1948, pp. 121, 125.

3. During the campaign Winston Churchill, a member of the Lloyd George government, had declared, "The Government policy is the nationalization of the railways. That great step it has at last been decided to take." (*Manchester Guardian,* December 5, 1918)

4. *TUC Annual Report, 1924,* pp. 350-351.

5. See *Labor Party Annual Report,* 1919, p. 156. *TUC Annual Report, 1919,* p. 74; G. D. H. Cole, *op. cit.*, pp. 395-396.

6. *Coal Industry Commission,* Coal Industry Commission Act, 1919; *Interim Report 20 March 1919* (London: HMSO Cmd 84), p. 5.

7. See *Coal Industry Commission,* Coal Industry Commission Act, 1919. *Second Stage Reports,* 20 June, 1919 (London, HMSO Cmd 210).

8. See *TUC Annual Report, 1920,* pp. 96, 109-112; also *British Trades Union Review,* October 1919 and December 1919.

9. See *British Trades Union Review,* March 1920, pp. 1-3.

10. Three months' production was lost in the stoppage of April through June 1921.

11. R. Page Arnot, *The Miners: Years of Struggle* (London: Allen and Unwin, 1935), p. 525.

12. Herbert Samuel, *The Problem of the Coal Mines* (London: Liberal Party Publications Dept. 1927), p. 3. See also the Report of the *Royal [Samuel] Commission on the Coal Industry* (1925), (London: HMSO Cmd. 2600, 1926), pp. 180-185.

13. The Miners' Federation in conjunction with the TUC, Labor Party and Parliamentary Labor Party between 1919 and 1926 advocated several plans for nationalization, with provisions for trade union representation in the management (i.e., "workers' control"), submitted in the form of legislation or as proposals to the several commissions which inquired into the coal industry.

14. *TUC Annual Report, 1925*, p. 158.

15. See *Cmd. 2600, op. cit.*, pp. 232-237.

16. *The Mining Crisis and the National Strike, 1926, Official Reports, Trades Union Congress* (London: Cooperative Printing Society, 1927), p. 83A.

17. Samuel, *The Problem of the Coal Mines, op. cit.*, p. 11.

CHAPTER III

1. Ministry of Transport, *Report of the Committee Appointed to Review the National Problem of the Supply of Electrical Energy*, May 1925. (London: HMSO, published March, 1926.)

2. Public corporation stock referred to here and subsequently is comparable to the debenture in the American corporate security terminology and involved no voting rights or alienation of the basic property of the corporation. Principal and interest were a general debt of the corporation and a charge on its revenue.

3. *Report of the Broadcasting Committee, 1925* (London: HMSO, Cmd. 2599, 1926).

4. *Report of the Commission of Inquiry Into Civil Aviation Appointed by the Prime Minister* (London: HMSO, Cmd. 5685, March, 1938).

5. See W.H.B. Court. Coal (*History of the Second World War; United Kingdom Civil Series*) London: HMSO, 1951, p. 22.

6. See *Court, op. cit.*, pp. 22-24.

7. *Ibid.*, pp. 27-28.

8. *TUC Annual Report, 1931*, p. 406.   9. *Ibid.*

10. *Ibid.*, pp. 433-436.   11. *Ibid.*, p. 346.

12. Reproduced in the *TUC Annual Report, 1932*, pp. 206-219.

13. *Ibid.*, p. 206.

14. Published under title *Tariffs and World Trade* (London: Trades Union Congress, 1932).

15. *TUC Annual Report, 1932*, p. 207.   16. *Ibid.*, p. 208.   17. *Ibid.*, p. 213.

18. *Ibid.*, p. 210.   19. *Ibid.*, p. 403.   20. *Ibid.*, p. 280.

21. *Ibid.*, p. 125.   22. *Labor Party Annual Report, 1932*, p. 215.

23. *Ibid.*, p. 213.

24. *Ibid.*, p. 224. The following year the TGWU reversed itself to support the National Executive Committee on the broad issue of "workers' control." During the debate Bevin after declaring "This . . . is primarily a trade union problem," went on to explain the TGWU position by saying that "This problem originally did not arise with Socialism at all . . . We in the Transport Workers' Union were faced with the problem of the immediate transfer of a large portion of the transport industry that was already under public control . . . In the process the principle on which we had acted for over forty years was denied to us in the establishment of the Board." (*Labor Party Annual Report, 1933*, p. 209).

25. *Labor Party Annual Report, 1932*, p. 224.

26. Reproduced in the *TUC Annual Report, 1933*, p. 210.

27. *Ibid.*   28. *Labor Party Annual Report, 1933*, pp. 205-206.

29. *TUC Annual Report, 1935*, p. 211.

30. *TUC Annual Report, 1944*, p. 439.

31. *TUC Annual Report, 1945*, p. 202.

32. *TUC Annual Report, 1946*, p. 218.

33. Reproduced in *TUC Annual Report, 1934*, pp. 189-205.

34. *Cotton; The TUC Plan for Socialization* (London: Cooperative Printing Society, 1935); partially reproduced in *TUC Annual Report, 1935*, pp. 202-208.

35. *Coal; The Labour Plan* (London: Cooperative Printing Society 1936); partially reproduced in the *TUC Annual Report, 1936*, pp. 210-13.

36. *TUC Annual Report, 1936*, pp. 214-220.

37. *Labor Party Annual Report, 1934*, pp. 253-255.

38. *TUC Annual Report, 1936*, p. 317.   39. *Ibid.*, pp. 162-163.

40. *TUC Annual Report, 1937*, pp. 154-155.   41. *Ibid.*, p. 198.

42. *Labor Party Annual Report, 1934*, pp. 247-249.   43. *Ibid.*, p. 247.

44. *TUC Annual Report, 1934*, p. 366. The TUC in 1936 gave more detailed expression to its policy towards Communism in the "British Labor Movement and Communism," (*TUC Annual Report, 1936*, pp. 225-230.)

45. *TUC Annual Report, 1936*, p. 221.

46. *TUC Annual Report, 1935*, pp. 217-224.

47. Quoted by Clive M. Schmitthoff in "The Nationalization of Basic Industries in Great Britain, *Law and Contemporary Problems*, Vol. XVI, No. 4, p. 557.

48. *Ministry of Fuel and Power; Statistical Digest 1946 and 1947* (London: HMSO, Cmd. 7548, November, 1948), p. 3.

49. Ministry of Fuel and Power, *Coal Mining, Report of the Technical Advisory Committee* (London: HMSO, Cmd. 6610, March, 1945), pp. 137-38.

50. Robert Foot, *A Plan for Coal, Being the Report to the Colliery Owners* (London: Mining Association of Great Britain, January 1945).

51. Ministry of Transport, *Report of the Committee on Electricity Distribution, May 1936* (London: HMSO, 1937), p. 81.

52. Ministry of Fuel and Power, *The Gas Industry,* Report of the Committee of Inquiry (London: HMSO, Cmd. 6699, December, 1945.)

53. Ministry of Civil Aviation, *British Air Transport* (London: HMSO, Cmd. 6605, March 1945).

54. Ministry of Civil Aviation, *British Air Services* (London: HMSO, Cmd. 6712, December 1945).

55. See Ministry of Town and Country Planning, *The Control of Land Use* (London: HMSO, Cmd. 6537, June 1944).

56. *The Economist* (London), June 30, 1945, p. 879.

57. *TUC Annual Report, 1940*, p. 365.   58. *Ibid.*, p. 330.

59. *TUC Annual Report, 1941*, p. 184.   60. *Ibid.*, p. 353.

61. *TUC Annual Report, 1942*, p. 123.   62. *Ibid.*, p. 39.

63. *TUC Annual Report, 1945*, p. 289.

64. *TUC Annual Report, 1942*, p. 125.

65. See the *Manchester Guardian*, December 4 and 5, 1941.

66. *TUC Annual Report, 1942*, p. 124.   67. *Ibid.*, pp. 284, 287-288.

68. *Ibid.*, pp. 283-284.   69. *TUC Annual Report, 1943*, pp. 146-147.

70. *TUC Annual Report, 1943,* p. 251. 71. *Ibid.,* p. 110.

72. Interdepartmental Committee on Social Insurance and Allied Services, *Social Insurance and the Allied Services,* report by Sir William Beveridge (London: HMSO Cmd. 6404, 1942).

73. Board of Education, *Educational Reconstruction* (London: HMSO Cmd. 6458, 1943).

74. *TUC Annual Report, 1943,* p. 236.

75. *TUC Annual Report, 1944,* p. 295. 76. *Ibid.,* pp. 393-443.

77. *Ibid.,* p. 436. 78. *Ibid.* 79. *Ibid.* 80. *Ibid.,* p. 439. 81. *Ibid.*

82. *Ibid.,* p. 401. 83. *Ibid.,* p. 437. 84. *Ibid.,* pp. 437-438.

85. *Ibid.,* p. 440. 86. *Ibid.,* p. 442. 87. *Ibid.*

88. *Ibid.,* p. 233; *Ministry of Works and Planning, Report of the Expert Commission on Compensation and Betterment* (London: HMSO Cmd. 6386, 1942).

89. *TUC Annual Report, 1944,* p. 308. 90. *Ibid.,* p. 377. 91. *Ibid.,* p. 379.

92. *Ibid.,* p. 306. 93. *TUC Annual Report, 1945,* p. 334.

94. In "Let Us Face the Future," the Labor Party defined its modified land policy this way in 1945: "Labour believes in land nationalization and will work towards it, but as a first step the State and local authorities must have wider and speedier powers to acquire land for public purposes wherever the public interest so requires. In this regard and for the purposes of controlling land use under town and country planning, we will provide for fair compensation, but we will also provide for a revenue for public funds from 'betterment'."

95. *TUC Annual Report, 1945,* p. 303.

96. *Ibid.,* p. 182; *TUC Annual Report, 1946,* p. 208.

97. Reproduced in the *TUC Annual Report, 1945,* pp. 504-526.

98. *Ibid.,* p. 504. 99. *Ibid.,* p. 506. 100. *Ibid.,* p. 507.

101. *Ibid.,* pp. 507-509. 102. *TUC Annual Report, 1945,* pp. 196-201.

103. *Ibid.,* p. 197. 104. *Ibid.,* p. 182. 105. *Ibid.,* p. 194.

106. *Ibid.,* p. 184. 107. *Ibid.,* p. 187. 108. *Ibid.* 109. *Ibid.,* p. 189.

110. *Ibid.,* p. 191. 111. *Ibid.* 112. *Ibid.,* pp. 527-542.

113. *Ibid.,* p. 527. 114. *Ibid.,* p. 528. 115. *Ibid.,* p. 394.

116. *TUC Annual Report, 1946,* p. 234.

CHAPTER IV

1. Sir Stafford Cripps in a written answer to a question in the House of Commons on March 16, 1949 stated: "On the basis of the total number of employees of industry, transport and communications in Great Britain at the middle of 1948, industries under public ownership at the present time represent about 17% of the total. The inclusion of gas, iron, and steel, and the balance of road transport would raise the percentage of public ownership to about 21 or 22."

Another estimate placed at almost 2 million or, 11-12% of all employees in Great Britain, the number working in the major enterprises nationalized after 1945, exclusive of steel. (See "Nationalised Industry," *Patterns of Organization in Nationalized Industry,* London: Acton Society Trust, 1951, p. 28).

2. For an account and analysis see W. A. Robson, *Problems of Nationalized*

Industry (New York: Oxford University Press, 1952), pp. 15-170. For a full-length detailed study of the measures of public ownership and control established by the Labor government see Robert A. Brady, *Crisis in Britain, Plans and Achievements of the Labour Government.* Berkeley: University of California Press, 1950.

3. *Forestry Act, 1945,* 8 and 9 Geo. 6 Chap. 35. *Forestry Act, 1947,* 10 and 11 Geo. 6, Chap. 21. *New Towns Act, 1946,* 9 and 10 Geo. 6, Chap. 68. *The Acquisition of Land Act, 1946* 9 and 10 Geo. 6, Chap. 49. *Agriculture Act, 1947,* 10 and 11 Geo. 6, Chap. 48. *Town and Country Planning Act, 1947,* 10 and 11 Geo. 6, Chap. 51. *The Water Act, 1948,* 11 and 12 Geo. 6, Chap. 22.

4. *National Insurance (Industrial Injuries) Act, 1946.* 9 and 10 Geo. 6, Chap. 62. *National Insurance Act, 1946,* 9 and 10 Geo. 6, Chap. 67. *National Health Service Act, 1946,* 9 and 10 Geo. 6, Chap. 81.

5. *Bank of England Act, 1946.* 9 and 10 Geo. 6, Chap 27.

6. *Coal Industry Nationalization Act, 1946,* 9 and 10 Geo. 6, Chap. 59.

7. *Civil Aviation Act, 1946,* 9 and 10 Geo. 6, Chap. 70.

8. *Cable and Wireless Act, 1946.* 9 and 10 Geo. 6, Chap. 82.

9. *Transport Act, 1947,* 10 and 11 Geo. 6, Chap. 49.

10. *Electricity Act, 1947.* 10 and 11 Geo. 6, Chap. 54.

11. *Gas Act, 1948.* 11 and 12 Geo. 6, Chap. 67.

12. *Iron and Steel Act, 1949.* 12 and 13 Geo. 6, Chap. 72.

13. *Cotton (Centralized Buying) Act, 1947.* 10 and 11 Geo. 6, Chap. 26

14. *Overseas Resources Development Act, 1948.* 11 and 12 Geo. 6, Chap. 15.

15. *Weekly Hansard,* No. 267, November 3-5, 1953. *The Economist* summed up: "Nationalization as a political issue has lost whatever power it had to sway votes. It is quite possible that there will be no more of it, even under a Labour Government; but it seems equally certain that the nationalized industries that now exist are here to stay. . . . For Labour and Tories alike, the policy ought to be to make the nationalized industries the objects of admiration, not contempt." ("Public Attitudes on Public Boards," *The Economist* July 21, 1956, p. 24).

16. *Iron and Steel Act, 1953.* 1 and 2 Eliz. 2, Chap. 15. The state, however, still retains considerable shareholdings in the industry.

17. *Transport Act, 1953.* 1 and 2 Eliz. 2, Chap. 13.

18. *Town and Country Planning Act, 1953.* 1 and 2 Eliz. 2, Chap. 16.

19. *Cotton Act, 1954.* 2 and 3 Eliz. 2, Chap. 24.

20. Prime Minister Winston Churchill explained his government's attitude at the 1953 Conservative Party conference as follows:

"The Conservative Government has adopted a sensible and practical policy toward what we found on becoming responsible. For the success of those industries like coal mining and railways, which we felt must remain nationalized, we have done and will continue to do our very best.

"But steel and transport, which had been so harshly struck at, we have liberated just in time. It will be proved in the next two years that this is greatly to the public advantage and convenience." (*New York Times,* October 11, 1953).

21. In discussing this possibility, R. H. S. Crossman, Labor M. P., and member of the Executive Committee of the Fabian Society and of the Executive Committee of the Labor Party, emphasized: "Actually the growth of a vast controlled State bureaucracy constitutes a grave potential threat to social democracy. The idea

that we are being disloyal to our Socialist principles if we attack its excesses or defend the individual against its incipient despotism is a fallacy." (R. H. S. Crossman, *Socialism and the New Despotism,* (London, Fabian Society 1956, p. 6.)

22. *TUC Annual Report, 1944,* p. 398.

23. Reproduced in the *TUC Annual Report for 1950,* pp. 564-575.

24. *Ibid.,* p. 564.   25. *Ibid.,* p. 575.

26. Reproduced in the *TUC Annual Report, 1953,* pp. 475-526.

27. In the case of nationalization of chemicals, the TUC was more reticent than the Labor Party which was on record for a "substantial degree of public ownership." The TUC report asked for "an inquiry into the facts" by a Labor government with a view to control. After, shifts back and forth at succeeding congresses, chemical nationalization disappeared from both the TUC and Labor Party programs. (*Ibid.,* pp. 514-515).

28. *Ibid.,* pp. 383-386.   29. *Ibid.,* p. 478.   30. *Ibid.,* pp. 249-257.

31. *Ibid.,* p. 254. Sir Lincoln Evans, general secretary of the Iron and Steel Trades Confederation, accepted the post of full-time Vice Chairman of the Iron and Steel Board. Messrs. J. Owen (National Union of Blastfurnacemen) and Sir Andrew Naesmith (Amalgamated Weavers' Association) were appointed part-time members. Mr. W. B. Beard (United Patternmakers' Association), after initially accepting a part-time appointment, resigned following the disapproval of the executive committee of his union. Replying to criticism for agreeing to participate in the administration of a denationalized industry, Evans wrote in his union's official journal in his capacity as general secretary: "Neither our loyalties to the Labour Party or its political needs require that trade unionists should refuse to serve on this Board. We would all have rightly criticized any act that did not provide for it. For to demand the opportunity and then, under pressure, to boycott it, would put the Trade Union Movement in an indefensible position and expose it to more discredit than the presence of any trade unionists on this Board could do." ("Trade Unions and the Steel Board," *Man and Metal,* Vol. XXX, June 1953, p. 100).

An opposing view was expressed by Ben Gardner, general secretary of the Amalgamated Engineering Union, who wrote in his union's official journal: "The Trade Union Movement in claiming the right to be consulted and its views considered by any and every government, surely did not mean that its assistance could be counted upon by a Government pursuing a policy to which the Movement is opposed. It is the responsibility, and the obligation of the trade unions to look after the interests of their members at all times and in all circumstances. These responsibilities extend to the political as well as the industrial sphere. And the unions cannot possibly exclude political considerations from the determination of policy in matters that are primarily of economic and industrial concern. It is really to falsify the history of our Movement to suggest that their attitude to a Labour Government must not be closer and more cooperative than with a Conservative Government." (*The Monthly Journal,* Amalgamated Engineering Union, Vol. XX, New Series No. 7, July 1953, pp. 193-194).

32. *Labor Party Annual Report, 1953,* p. 125.

33. *TUC Annual Report, 1955,* p. 417.   34. *Ibid.,* p. 420.

35. *TUC Annual Report, 1956,* pp. 296-297.

36. *TUC Annual Report, 1957,* p. 457.

37. *TUC Annual Report, 1958,* p. 455. See also *Ibid.,* pp. 298-302 and pp. 349-358.

38. *Labor Party Annual Report, 1946,* p. 124.

39. *Labor Party Annual Report, 1955,* p. 170.   40. *Ibid.,* p. 173.

41. *Ibid.,* p. 174-175. Gaitskell, who was chosen leader of the Parliamentary Labour Party in December 1955, later elaborated his ideas on the place of public ownership of industry in a mixed economy and made the point: "Anybody who thinks about it for a moment will agree that nationalization, which is an institutional change in the ownership and control of industry must be treated as a means and not grouped with the ultimate aims [of socialism] which I have just described. The fact that it is nevertheless often treated as an end, as, indeed more or less identical with Socialism, is because it has been regarded not as a means to achieve the ideals of Socialism, but as the *only possible* means *which could not fail to produce the desired ends.*" (sic) (See Hugh Gaitskell, *Socialism and Nationalization,* London, Fabian Society, 1956, p. 5.)

The Labour Party Constitution, as of 1957, still stated as one of its objects, Clause IV (4): "To secure for the workers by hand or by brain the full fruits of their industry and the most equitable distribution thereof that may be possible, upon the basis of the common ownership of the means of production, distribution, and exchange, and the best obtainable system of popular administration and control of each industry and service. (*Labor Party Annual Report, 1955,* p. 234)

42. *National Superannuation: Labour's Policy for Security in Old Age,* (London: Labor Party, 1957).

43. *Public Enterprise, Labour's Review of the Nationalized Industries,* (London: Labor Party, 1957). *Industry and Society, Labor's Policy on Future Public Ownership,* (London: Labor Party, 1957).

44. *Public Enterprise, op. cit.,* p. 22.

45. *Ibid.,* p. 56.   46. *Ibid.*

47. *Industry and Society, op. cit.,* p. 59   48. *Ibid.*

49. *Ibid., pp.* 32-34.   50. *Ibid.,* p. 39

51. *Ibid.,* p. 40: *National Superannuation, op. cit.,* pp. 100-101.

52. *Industry and Society, op. cit.,* p. 47   53. *Ibid.,* pp. 46-47.

54. *Ibid.,* p. 47.   55. *Ibid.,* p. 50

56. *Ibid.,* p. 52   57. *Ibid.,* p. 56.

58. *Ibid.,* pp. 40-41.

59. What may be considered as exceptions to this interpretation are machine tools, housing, and water supply. The TUC is committed to a general statement that the "Congress believes that the greater part of the machine tool industry should be brought under public ownership." (*TUC Annual Report, 1957,* p. 453). The Labor Party has accepted this view in conjunction with its own policy on automation. Both bodies also are broadly committed to extend municipally-owned housing and to integrate the remaining privately-operated water supply companies into publicly-owned systems. (See *Labor Party Annual Report, 1957,* pp. 216 and 134, respectively).

60. *Labor Party Annual Report, 1957,* p. 157.

61. *Prosper the Plough,* a Policy for a Sound and Efficient British Agriculture (London, Labor Party, 1958).

62. *Labor Party Annual Report, 1958,* p. 133.

63. *Learning to Live,* A Policy for Education from Nursery School to University, (London, Labor Party, 1958).

64. *Plan for Progress,* Labour's Policy for Britain's Economic Expansion, (London, Labor Party, 1958).

65. *Ibid.,* p. 43.

66. *Ibid.,* p. 56. The policy statement on automation promised at the 1957 Labor Party conference (when an interim report was approved) was not issued on the grounds that developments in this field had not advanced sufficiently for a final statement to be made. *Ibid.,* p. 3.

67. *Your Personal Guide to The Future Labor Offers You,* (London, Labor Party, 1958).

INDEX